STARS OF HEAVEN
MYSTICAL ASTROLOGY

HOLY ORDER OF MANS

Published by Holy Order of MANS
Corte Madera, California

Cover and interior layout and design by Carolyn Oakley, Luminous Moon Design + Press, Boulder, Colorado

First Edition
First Printing: October 2023

ISBN-13: 979-8-9889669-1-3

Body, Mind & Spirit: Astrology — Body, Mind & Spirit: Mysticism — Body, Mind & Spirit: Alchemy

Printed and bound in the United States of America

OTHER PUBLICATIONS BY
HOLY ORDER OF MANS

The Golden Force
Keystone of the Tarot with Meditations
Jewels of the Wise: Self-Mastery Through the Tarot
Tarot 22 Keys – The Major Arcana (tarot card coloring set)
The Discovery

FORTHCOMING

Tree of Life

DEDICATION

*For those who wish to discover and understand the
Map of the Universe hidden within themselves.*

Stars of Heaven: Mystical Astrology

ACKNOWLEDGMENTS

Stars of Heaven: Mystical Astrology was originally published by the Holy Order of MANS in 1967. By the late 1980's the Holy Order of MANS came apart and, consequently, their books were no longer available.

A heartfelt thank you to Helen Blighton for her diligent work on the Order publications in the 1960's, and again in the 2000's. Special thanks to Mark and Mary Anderson of the Science of Man who created a website in the 1990's and made these Order books available online. Special thanks to those who continued to do the Work of the Order during this time; and to Mary Ray who took on the daunting task of retyping most of the Order literature, including this book, in the mid 1990's, and putting it on the website www.HolyOrderOfMANS.org. Special thanks to Margot Whitney, Director, Holy Order of MANS who, in 2012, resurrected the Holy Order of MANS for the 21st century. Thank you to Carolyn Oakley at Luminous Moon Design for her patience and talented work designing and laying out the book and cover, and Shawn Collins for his expert Astrological knowledge. And thank you to Michael Maciel, Director, Holy Order of MANS for his contributions toward the publication of this book.

Most importantly, and with heartfelt gratitude, we've placed our trust in God.

"...and Jesus looking upon them saith, 'With men it is impossible, but not with God; for with God all things are possible.' " (Mark 10:27)

INTRODUCTION

The purpose of this book is not to show you how to set up or read a horoscope. Such information can be found in many books. But here we seek to help you get acquainted with the feeling and personality of signs and planets and their underlying symbology.

We assure you that although astrological charts are based on a concept which places the earth at the center of the wheel, this does not render them invalid, as the study of an individual chart would show. This is because the average man/woman is the center of their own universe, which seems to revolve around them. As far as earthman is concerned in his daily physical needs, the sun and moon encircle his environment to bring him night and day, cycles and seasons.

It is only when he passes beyond the self-centered area of consciousness to become a solar-oriented being, a true Sun-Son, that he moves, in essence, off the wheel of earth's Karma and consciousness to join with the great Identity at the center of the solar system. Then he no longer wishes to categorize himself within the limits of a zodiacal pattern, which was manifest at the time his present vehicle emerged. In becoming one with God, he identifies with the timeless essence of his true Being, and thus partakes of all these twelve attributes as One.

The Holy Order of MANS is an organization dedicated to a more thorough understanding of the universal laws of the Creator so that all might better manifest God's Creation and thus promote Peace and Harmony among people everywhere. Our purpose is to teach the Ancient Christian wisdom to this new generation as it was taught in the past.

Our organization is called the Holy Order of MANS because the universal laws of creation, the law of prayer, and other principles can be taught and, in your everyday life, you can become the master of your fate through conscious application of these principles.

We use the term "man" to include both men and women.

CONTENTS

Our Divine Mother has fashioned a marvelous gown
the deep blue of an evening sky.
Its fabric through the mighty Ages
has been interwoven with whispered fables
and myths wrought by every creature of heaven and earth,
of Time and Space, of angels, gods and men.

Fine patterns they trace
like a Documentary of Time
on the misty folds of her gracefully flowing garb.

She is the Sea in which our Island Earth floats by
along with other orbs—all sparkling jewels
which flash with every movement of her thought,
and dance with gentle rhythm in the beauty of the Night.

The Moon is Her pendant, and the Sun Her Crown;
and She both day and night enwraps the worlds around,
remembering, as the Soul remembers All.

CREATION

"Let there be lights in the firmament of the heavens to separate the day from the night, and let them be for signs and for seasons, and for days and years." (Genesis 1:14)

In the beginning, before worlds or beings or creatures, there was naught but seeming space. This space was filled with the powers and forces of God, but It needed to be ordered to become constructive and beneficent. So the Great Intelligence of God organized these powers through sending forth of the Word, that the essence of the powers in Sound might control the forces of the Universe. Where the Father centers His Great Consciousness the processes of Creation take place.

The starry systems have evolved from unformed gaseous masses in space, which are the first substances evolving from pure energy, these being made up of positive and negative units of electricity. Through gravitation these masses settled into a compact area and began to have a sort of transparent substance, like a nebulous sphere.

The nature of this energy causes rotation of the sphere, which in gathering speed becomes elongated like a spindle. As several of these nebulae whirl simultaneously there occurs a sort of tidal force or pull which detaches parts from the whole, and separates these into individual whirling masses which become stars.

The rising speed of acceleration also causes increase of heat and light, and bits of substance fly off the surface into space to become more stars. This same principle holds true in forming the planets, as smaller amounts detach from the stars and at some distance away begin to cool and solidify into denser form, becoming planets, or satellites of planets. The tidal pull of various bodies upon each other holds them in suitable position clustered at balanced distances apart to move around stronger bodies whose gravitational pull holds them in course as they whirl into orderly systems of galaxies and universes.

The word *galaxy* is from the Greek word *gala*, which means "milk." Our own galaxy is called the Milky Way because the thick sprinkling of luminous stars gives a white, milky effect in the sky. This galaxy is of wheel formation, with thicker places like hubs at the center where the Great Nucleus is located. As you look past the general direction of Sagittarius in the heavens there can be seen a thicker area of stars beyond which this Nucleus lies. Around this great sun revolves our own entire solar system along with millions of others. As you look at the thinner portion of the Milky Way in the sky, you are looking at its lengthwise part, which thins out in density toward the rim, away from the Nucleus.

This galaxy is revolving around an even larger Center, somewhere beyond the Virgo area, but at such distance and size as cannot concern the human mind. We must work with our own solar system, and look to the Lord thereof to translate for us anything beyond Its sphere. Wheels within wheels, cycles within cycles; small orbits within larger orbits, all within vaster orbits beyond human comprehension.

Ezekiel had a vision of the Chariot of Jehovah, surrounded by a whirlwind of clouds and flames; the ancient mystics have called this Chariot a symbol of the whole solar system, while its wheels represent the orbits of the planets.

The distances between stars run into numbers so "astronomical" when given in miles, that their distances are more simply measured in light years—that is the length of time it takes *light* to travel from star to star. This is at the speed of 186,000 miles per second, or nearly six million, million miles per one light year. So when we say Arcturus is 33 light years away, this would be difficult to signify or even imagine in terms of miles.

When people ask how distant stars and planets can have any effect on human beings, let us remind you just as a curiosity, that the 1933 World's Fair was officially opened by allowing a beam from distant Arcturus to turn on the switch.

The actual constellations we see in the sky are not clusters of stars all together in one group or system. They relate to each other only in the sense that all are in a single line of vision as one gazes at any given section of the heavens. Actually, they are those stars inhabiting certain regions mapped out by astronomers, the 48 original star-groups described by Ptolemy having now been expanded to number 88 constellations recognized by today's astronomers.

These star groupings become useful in helping to find or describe the location of planets and other celestial bodies. When we say Altair is in Aquila, it is like saying a map would show Lincoln to be in Nebraska. The charting of stars is most useful in navigation on the high seas, where there are no identifying road-marks, except those in the heavens, to show direction.

Some astronomers claim the Euphrates Valley as the place where the constellations of the "zodiac" (literally "circle of animals") was named. Their present arrangement indicates the time of their naming was the Taurean Age, roughly somewhere between 4698 B.C. and 2540 B.C. (no definite agreement has been reached as to the boundary dates of the Ages).

Since the Great Pyramid is located at the exact center of the world's land area, its building is logically assumed as the middle of the Age of the fixed Earth sign, Taurus. In ancient times the Earth was considered the center of the universe. The consciousness of many persons still would seem to place it there.

The ancient priests of Egypt and Mesopotamia first mapped out the heavens into twelve divisions, beginning at the point where the sun (as it appeared to them) crossed the ecliptic at the vernal equinox.

This is the date when day and night are of equal length, as the sun swings upward to bring longer, warmer days.

Of course, we know the Sun doesn't move in relation to us. It only moves in relation to those larger systems with which we have no concern at all, except curiosity. But it is simpler, from our point of view, to map it as though it were moving around us.

In relation to us, the sun stands relatively still, somewhat as a shepherd leading his flocks, while we, like sheep, move round and round him, along with the other planets. He moves also on a larger yearly cycle, his long, slow trek taking us through meadows and mountains, in a great circle in search of grassy pasture, and returning to the barn only at midwinter, carrying his flock like a miniature solar system along with him.

These sheep might think the whole world, including the shepherd, was revolving around them, but actually they would only be circling round him in his steady yearly path. He also would be moving in some still larger pattern of life relating to things in his own human environment, beyond the comprehension or concern of the sheep.

However, distance dilutes the effects of things, so we actually receive most impact from that which is near to us. Lest the scope of creation make you feel too minute and insignificant, remember that you too are lord of your own universe. Not only do you have a central nucleus in the Self, and exude an atmosphere around you, but you also affect other persons through interchange of magnetism and radiation. Above all your mind has the power to direct and create new conditions in your life and environment. The cells of your body are living, conscious entities which respond to your thoughts and feelings and react to your direction. These are totally dependent upon your state of consciousness.

Man's soul is of the same components as the stars, but he must learn to master and guide the influences of this soul, even as the Supreme Being guides the stars in their courses.

His vital body is of the same ethereal substance as that of suns and stars, bringing him into sympathy with them so that they attract something from man, and he from them. But he must learn to accept only influences he desires to have affect him.

Herewith lies the ancient teaching that "man must rule his stars," not be ruled by them. Astrology as part of the wisdom teachings has always maintained that man has free will, and makes his own destiny. Only charlatans would indicate to anyone that he is under stern restriction of Fate. It is true everyone carries into this incarnation certain Karmic situations caused by things done or experienced in previous lives, of debts contracted and rewards earned. But none of these things rules tomorrow. Only what he does, says, and thinks today has authority over the future, both the patterns of this life and of those to come.

The horoscope is not a magic formula, but a map of the heavens exactly as it appeared at the moment of birth. That is all, but its imprint was to some extent sealed upon the infant personality at that moment. He could not have the same horoscope in another incarnation, since there will be no repetition of this pattern before 26,000 years, where all the planets will be in the same positions. The being goes on through a series of different horoscopes as it does bodies, the soul remaining ever the same, except that it evolves and grows through the many experiences given it for that purpose, until it comes to recognize its own divinity and responsibility to its Creator, and then it won't need the lessons any more. You do not belong to any sign of the Zodiac, you only use their attributes as given, for the time being, and potentially have use of them all.

At birth is shown the essence of characteristics predominant in the individual at that moment. It may have been that certain attributes, habits, or faults, were concentrated in this particular incarnation to help him work them off more speedily. In any case, he should never leave this earth plane the same as he entered it, lest his whole opportunity for growth and reason for being here be wasted. He changes yearly, almost daily, so we know he is never just as the horoscope found him as a baby entering the earth plane.

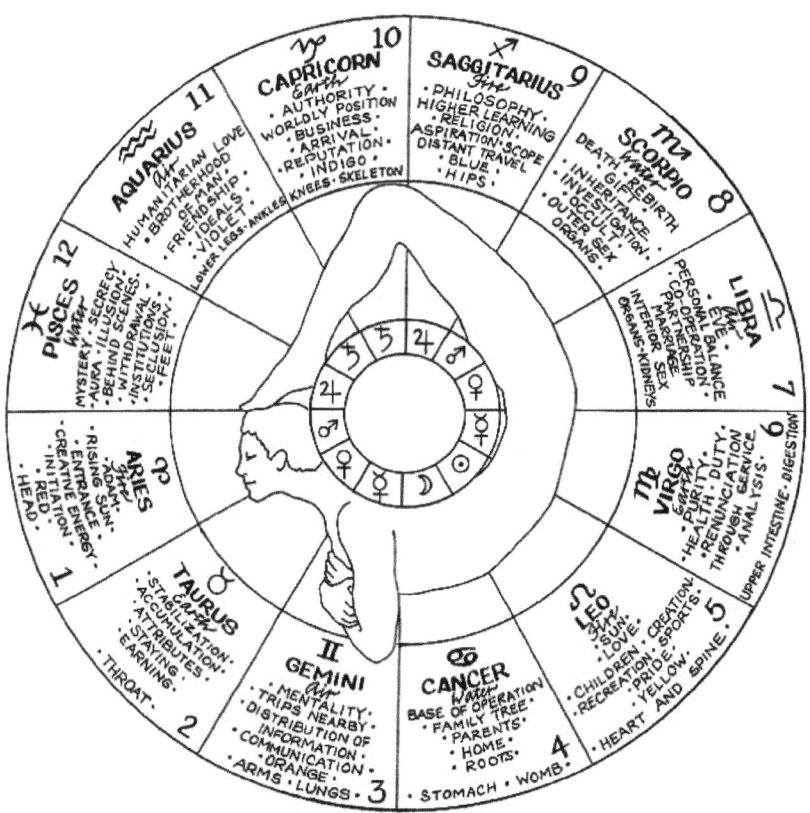

EVOLUTION OF EARTH & MAN

The accompanying chart shows the planets being thrown off from the Sun, using the point between Leo and Cancer as the symbolical matrix or point of birth, between the two Lights of the Sun and Moon.

If we take man himself as passing through the same super-cycles and going through a process of evolution similar to that of the earth, though with different timing, he would have assumed Life and come forth into the dawn of…

…Light between the womb of Cancer and the Life-giving Sun/Son of Leo. He would have been at this time a "misty" but happy creature, living by feeling and instinct, not far from God in inner communication.

On either side of Cancer and Leo is a sign ruled by Mercury—that is Gemini and Virgo. This is the closest visible planet to the Sun. So man's next step would have been to develop mind and mental attributes. This gives independence, and beginning to listen less to the inner voice, more to the outer.

On either side of the Mercury signs are Taurus and Libra, ruled by Venus. So love blossomed as man grew and increased, along with beauty and complications. He probably tended more toward vegetarianism then, and worship of female goddesses.

Earth itself fills this space…

Next come the Mars-ruled signs Aries and Scorpio (very recently was Pluto discovered). Here entered aggressive action, planning and carrying out of activities, making of laws. Here were pioneering, hunting, and eating meat, fighting over conflicting interests, and finding medicine to patch wounds. Male gods.

* * * Where there should be a planet is a belt of asteroids * * *

The next planet is the largest of all, Jupiter. It is a planet of expansion and improvement, of looking-up to formulate religious concepts, to prophesy, and to develop philosophical ideas. It is a time of travel, of spreading out, and improving living conditions. Sagittarius and Pisces. Man was unaware of the existence of Neptune, while going through this.

Saturn completes the circle, ruling Capricorn and Aquarius (before the discovery of Uranus). Mankind is only now entering this phase. Saturn was the outermost of the planets formerly known. But now we are aware of the one beyond, Uranus, which has broken through the boundary line, and expanded our consciousness.

PRECESSION OF EQUINOXES

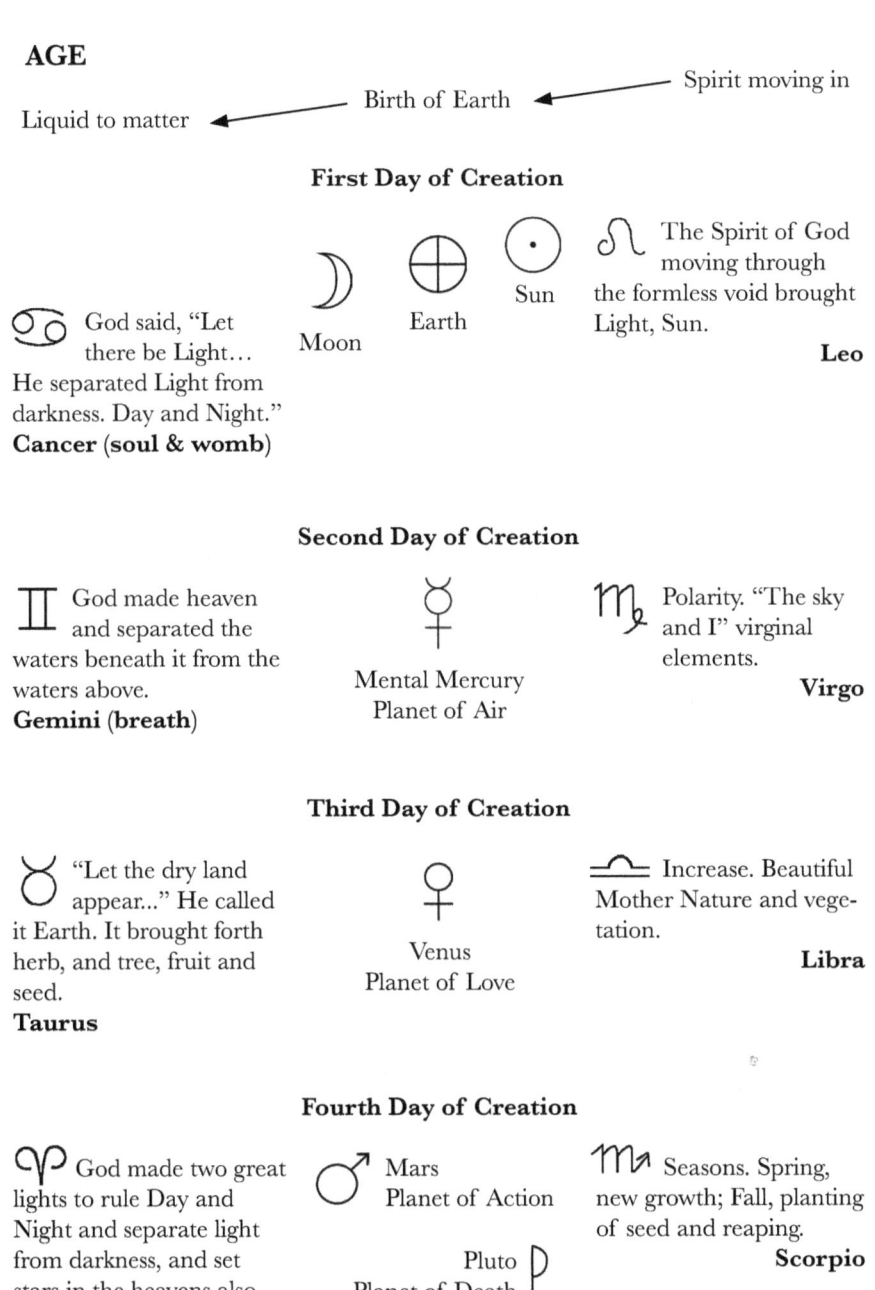

AGE

Spirit moving in

Birth of Earth

Liquid to matter

First Day of Creation

God said, "Let there be Light... He separated Light from darkness. Day and Night."
Cancer (soul & womb)

Moon

Earth

Sun

The Spirit of God moving through the formless void brought Light, Sun.
Leo

Second Day of Creation

God made heaven and separated the waters beneath it from the waters above.
Gemini (breath)

Mental Mercury
Planet of Air

Polarity. "The sky and I" virginal elements.
Virgo

Third Day of Creation

"Let the dry land appear..." He called it Earth. It brought forth herb, and tree, fruit and seed.
Taurus

Venus
Planet of Love

Increase. Beautiful Mother Nature and vegetation.
Libra

Fourth Day of Creation

God made two great lights to rule Day and Night and separate light from darkness, and set stars in the heavens also.
Aries

Mars
Planet of Action

Pluto
Planet of Death

Seasons. Spring, new growth; Fall, planting of seed and reaping.
Scorpio

Fifth Day of Creation

♓ "Let waters bring forth swarms of living creatures, and birds fly across the heavens…"
Pisces

♆ Neptune
Mystic

Jupiter ♃
Philosophy,
Religion, Plenty

♐ Sea power and ships of Neptune/ Pisces; psychic. Philosophy and travel.
Sagittarius

Sixth Day of Creation

♒ "Let Earth bring forth living creatures, beasts and things that creep on the ground." Then He made man to have dominion over all the rest.
Aquarius

♅ Uranus
Change & Invention

Saturn ♄
Government

♑ The age of Man learning his powers of dominion over all forces and self.
Capricorn

SIGNS OF THE ZODIAC

HOUSES

The first six houses express things of more immediate or personal application, whereas the seventh through twelfth houses indicate more of a desire to share experience with others.

In this way the last six houses seem a projection outward of the first six.

First House: *I am, I do.*
Second House: *I have.*
Third House: *I think.*
Fourth House: *I establish roots.*
Fifth House: *I love you.*
Sixth House: *I will serve you.*

Seventh House: *We can do more together.*
Eighth House: *Let us share.*
Ninth House: *What do great ones think?*
Tenth House: *I establish prestige.*
Eleventh House: *All are my brothers.*
Twelfth House: *I renounce all for service.*

ARIES
(Approximately March 21 – April 20)
First Sign – Ruled by Mars

Once the **Aries** person has found God, he lets nothing else be placed first, and becomes an ardent, shining Knight of the Spirit, with but one sworn purpose.

"Aries" means "a ram," the constellation being named for the Ram with the Golden Fleece in Greek mythology. This Fleece is sometimes called the "wool of the wise," pulled over the eyes of the foolish.

In ancient Mystery Schools, the Wisdom teachings and rites of Aries were celebrated at a temple in the Libyan desert dedicated to Jupiter-Ammon, who was shown with a ram's horn upon his forehead. Michelangelo also depicted Moses with horns, significantly, for Moses lived during the Arian Age.

The symbol for Aries is drawn like the nose and horns of a ram, the male or head-sheep, leader of the flock. His nose thrusts forward as for encounter or discovery, with the horns upward and outward in aggressive, extrovert motion.

The symbol also is shaped like a young, green plant of corn sprouting upward in Spring, the vertical line showing two divergent semi-circles, or half-moons, drawn together at the base into oneness and unity of action.

This is indicative of the first appearance of form, coming forth to express in matter, or the place where spirit and matter begin to perform as one unit. It is the point of outward beginning of conscious life, the hatching forth of the egg from its protective shell, or the reaching-out of life to extend new green fingertips from the end of every branch and put flowers on every twig.

Here we see resurrection of Life out of the husks of winter, when that which seemed dead is found once again and eternally alive.

Life is kindled in Aries, driven by the creative Power of the Life Force—a gravity-defying Force which must push ever upward, the Cosmic Principle of Individuality, challenging all obstacles, and defying all odds.

To Mars, the planet of Life-Principle and source of energy, has been assigned the rulership of Aries, as a suitable channel through which his energy can be expressed. The Sun is exalted in Aries, and here the warrior Mars is transformed into the radiant Son. It is a hot, dry, positive and masculine sign.

Enter with Aries! The Zodiac is measured from the Vernal Equinox, or first point of Aries, where the Sun crosses northward over the celestial equator, and marks the beginning of Spring. In the horoscope this point corresponds with the Eastern horizon, or place where the sun daily rises, and is named the Ascendant or rising sign.

Aries rules the head, and especially the eyes, of the physical body, those windows from which the soul peers out to discern life. It is the head which rules the body and makes the decisions. Aries has been known as the Capstone of the twelve signs and the cerebral activity of the Spiritual Fire.

It is the first of the cardinal, or leading, signs of the Zodiac, representing the power of identity. As head of the Fire Trinity, Aries is the Archetype of Fire and the leading principle thereof. "I am the Way," Jesus says. His is the dynamic courageous urge to thrust forward into life, with irradiating irresistible force.

This is a sign of male power and martial energy, swift in action. Being a primal force of simple, crude energy, it corresponds with the vigor of the first "red-blooded" man, Adam.

Negatively, he may become rash, combative or restless. His natural aggression is good for leadership, but he must guard against bossiness and must learn patience and self-control.

❦

First House — Red on the Color Wheel
"I am the Good Shepherd"

The first house is also the Ascendant, or rising sign of the horoscope, as the sign coming up over the eastern horizon at the moment and place of birth.

It represents the *"I,"* the person himself as he expresses outwardly or appears to others. This is the house of personality and of the vehicle or physical appearance, general condition of the body and mannerisms—the envelope in which the Self is placed. It depicts the active *approach* of the individual toward life—the Fire of Life; the Creative Energy and Vitality.

It is an aggressive and pioneering sign, as the place of beginnings, spearheading a drive into new areas of personal development.

The first house also depicts generally the conditions of early childhood years.

TAURUS
(Approximately April 20 – May 21)
Second Sign – Ruled by Venus

Taurus is one of the raw forces with which Creation began—being among the first three Logoi. It represents primeval Earth, or the Archetype of Earth, as the Fixed and most solid form thereof.

Here is carried the Principle of Cosmic Stability, where Life accumulates Power and develops an enduringly productive attitude, carried forth as an urge for material sustenance and security.

The Taurean person requires certain lessons and experiences having to do with finances or possessions, and he must learn the correct use of the energies and products of earth so that he becomes not bound by them, nor turned aside by the word *mine*. His "goods" must not become gods.

The word *Taurus* means "the Bull." So also, the letter-word for what we call A, the first letter of the alphabet of the Middle Eastern nations, translates as "Ox" or "Bull." It is believed the alphabet came into existence during the Age of Taurus, when the Bull was worshipped as a divine symbol and logically given first place.

The Egyptians paid homage to a sacred bull, Apis, considered as the representative of their god Osiris. Apis, in Egyptian, means "the hidden." The ancient Mysteries of Serapis were in celebration of the rites of Taurus. A tomb was dedicated also to "the Heavenly Bull;" and around that time the cow became sacred in India.

The symbol which represents this sign is shown as a circle surmounted by a semi-circle, or a crescent moon resting on a globe. The Moon is exalted in Taurus, the sign of Mother Earth, although Venus is the actual ruler of the sign. Their combined influence aids in the unfoldment of instinct.

The empty circle of this symbol pictures the great feminine creative potential, the upturned half-circle being receptive to Spirit, like a cup lifted to obtain from the Source all things needed for growth and to retain that which is received.

The symbol also looks like the round face and incurved horns of a bull and, like its appearance, is much less aggressive than Aries, being of a more settled and stolid nature.

Cattle have long been used to till the soil, to haul burdens and turn mills, as well as to furnish milk and meat to sustain the children of men. Their strong digestive powers and slow chewing of the cud aptly picture the deliberate composure of this sign.

Their muscular necks emphasize the strength of the throat, neck and voice-box, all of which Taurus rules. The primordial desire-force of its ruling planet, Venus, whose latent power has been stored in a reservoir of force, must be transformed into spiritual power. This force can be compressed and contained just so long, and then it irresistibly bursts forth in Song. Here is held the secret of Sound and manifestation of the vocalizing power of speech.

The Bull represents the fertility of Nature and the natural resources of Earth at the call of Spirit. This soul-source of Power is like unto one who plants, cultivates and patiently watches his garden bloom. For it is a sign of agriculture and of herdsmen; especially was this so when the world was young and man lived a simple life close to Nature.

This sign represents the reward for labor and the storage of earthly goods and of Life-forces. The Taurean is usually uncomplicated, with excellent health, is steadfast in affection and self-reliant in his search for security. His are the gifts of simplicity and natural beauty.

He will hold to peace at any price until pushed to extremes, when he may become like a raging bull. But he is normally unruffled, tolerant and very practical. He likes good food and furnishings, yet must not let the weight of gravity pull him into a rut nor forget what is the true spiritual foundation. He must avoid stubbornness and tyranny.

This is a fixed, feminine Earth sign—a pillar of strength to family and loved ones.

Second House — Color: Red-Orange

"Lay up for yourselves treasures in heaven..."

The keynote of the second house is found in the word "mine," for here the emphasis is upon the sense of ownership, or point of possession, of natural assets and accumulations.

The earning potential or capacity is shown here, as well as various resources gained or saved by one's own efforts. Herewith is the stabilization of all means of earthly support and the media of exchange, as stocks, bonds, loans and banks.

It is a place not only of purchasing power, but of *earthly power*, and of the building of form.

It is a place not only of financial accruements, but the savings in the soul-bank of *talents* as we use the term today; skills and attributes developed in this life or before are part of the portion of this house. It is a place of abilities and blessings. Here are especially the vocal attributes, the speaking or singing voice.

GEMINI
(Approximately May 21 – June 21)
Third Sign – Ruled by Mercury

The symbol for **Gemini** is fashioned like two pillars, or as two ways from which to choose. The Gemini person must stand between these two polarities of positive and negative, which may cause certain indecision and restlessness.

The Twins, symbolic of Gemini, are named Castor and Pollux after the twin sons of Jupiter in mythology and two bright stars in the constellation Gemini. The rites of Gemini were held at Samothrace, where ceremonial hymns were sung to Castor and Pollux.

The pillars also refer to Adam and Eve; the dark pillar at left shows the *knowledge* which stems from earth and intellect, while the light pillar at right refers to the *wisdom* of sense-free spiritual Truth. The dark side is referred to Eve as fashioner of form and the white to the masculine principle of Creative Fire.

One may make a wise choice between good and evil when knowledge is perfected concerning the union of spirit and matter, when all things are seen as one whole, and facts are gathered not from the outer rim of things, but from the Center of Source.

Physically, Gemini rules the hands, arms, lungs and shoulders— the breathing apparatus. Two arms and two lungs further bring out the idea of duality, this knowledge of differences whereby each part must be brought into the whole. Such versatility makes difficult any single-minded application to a single idea, job or personal situation.

As intellect, Gemini is the third of the Logoic Triad. It is the Archetype of the element Air, which abounds freely for all without question of good or bad. Its function is Cosmic Distinctiveness, wherein is seen the purpose of all things, however minute.

Into this sign where Divine Ideas take shape, Life flows almost playfully from the first two. These first three signs relate more to the Abstract, or Fundamental Planes of Creation, rather than to Nature and Man as we encounter them.

Mercury is counted as the ruler of Gemini—this messenger of the gods who was swift and mercurial, of great wit and cunning. He was also clever enough to use his hands as a thief. In addition, his too-clever tongue is unwisely used in lies, whether to gain a dishonest end, or in contempt of a mind less swift because it is occupied in another direction. He may be two-faced as well as two-armed, changing colors like a chameleon according to whom he encounters, or bearing tales from one to another. He should avoid becoming bored, jumping from job to job, or from experience to experience.

His probing instinct is toward experience, but even more toward all communication. He likes diversion, is "volatile as air, and mobile as quick-silver." One of his best features is his ability to adapt and adjust, both to his environment and to other people, being most versatile as well as genial, humane and democratic.

His inquisitive intellect may make him charming, or even brilliant, as a scientist, teacher or writer. He is gifted with eloquence of expression which should not be wasted in small talk. His detachment should not become cruelty or cynicism. He is usually unbiased, able to see both sides and to relate to the common mind. His easy charm and restless mobility may prove somewhat shallow in affections or sympathies.

There is love of detail and appreciation of the distinctions and differences of unlike things. This interest in inter-relationships is brought out again in Gemini's rulership over brothers, sisters and neighbors—as well as of all sorts of communications, whether by writing, speaking or taking short journeys to make contact either in personal or business matters. This brings out the Gemini rulership over office work, newspapers, mail and telephone, and modes of transportation: the distribution of information.

◐~

Third House — Orange on the Color Wheel
"As a man thinketh in his heart, so is he..."

This is the mercurial house of thought, the place of inquiry, of brain, intellect and mentality.

Small and swift as Mercury's orbit around the sun, the third house concentrates on nearby associations such as neighbors and brethren, or on short journeys to nearby areas. It is concerned with thoughts and things near at hand.

Communication, or the exchange of thought, is important here. All messages, whether by email, text, cell phone, social media, newspaper or periodical are handled. The acquisition and distribution of information, writing and literary skill are ruled by this house.

It rules all papers, deeds or documents, as well as office activity. It also holds sway in the field of commerce, in motion and change. It is dual and distinctive; thus, here one learns to choose.

CANCER
(Approximately June 21 – July 23)
Fourth Sign – Ruled by Moon

The symbol shows twin forces, those of involution and of evolution, but in seed form, not fully unfolded; rather the inner terminals are curled in little balls, like twin centers of energy or miniature suns, which by their distance apart generate a flow of attraction of Life-Force between which develops the Matrix of Life.

The semi-circles are shaped like two crescent moons, the Moon being called the ruler of **Cancer**. These have also been designated as cups or chalices, one up-turned to receive the flow from above, the other pouring out to give. The small circles have been called both seeds and breasts. True, Cancer represents the Mother Principle, ruling in the physical body the breasts, the stomach and womb, all related to nourishment, sustenance and shelter.

The mother influence is ever the nourisher of immature growth, where the tenderness of reflected light is more beneficial than the direct glare of the Sun too soon. Thus, the Mother becomes an intermediary link between child and world.

Along with this natural urge to nourish and protect may come a sensitive or defensive attitude. Cancerians must guard against distrust of the motives of others or favoritism toward those closer by personal relationship or responsibility. Though they start out loving family first, the evolved Cancerian extends this to town, country and, finally, the whole world.

Like the constellation itself, which does not blaze ostentatiously, Cancer tends to be the most inconspicuous of all signs, somewhat retiring in nature. Yet inwardly they may be torn between the desire to become invisible and the wish to be more recognized and appreciated. They are actually ever-changing, if circumstances allow, and may take on more than one identity during a lifetime. Sometimes the acting profession becomes an outlet for this tendency.

In the constellation shines an interesting cluster of stars called the Beehive. Cancer was called by Chaldean philosophers the Gate of Men, considered as the sign in which the soul entered the body. In any case, it is the place where life begins on the inner levels, before it becomes manifest, and is nurtured into birth and growth. The Moon forces perfect the body, giving physical form to life.

Cancer is the sign relating to Soul, in touch always with the Cosmic Subconscious or Oversoul, with the Divine Mother of Heaven. This stage represents form in its fluidic state, before solidification.

As fourth sign of the Zodiac, the first square aspect is formed— that of Cancer to Aries, a 90-degree or quarter-circle aspect. Aries, being the more aggressive of the two, causes in Cancer a more inward or occult activity. The Aries-Cancer aspect may produce psychic sensitivity or mediumship, being in close harmony with the astral worlds through mutual rulership by the moon.

This square, while the foundation of form, as represented by the number four, is also somewhat stripped of the "rude energy" found in Aries, thus less strong, as here at its place of entrance into form, the soul first becomes conscious of limitation. Cancer is the second Cardinal sign, a feminine Water sign,

Basically kind, emotional and intuitive, Cancerians tend to reflect moods, and must be careful that these are positive, for like the Moon of ever-changing phases, they tend to swing from one mood to another with the changing tides of inner or outer life. This constant rhythmic pattern of the Moon's activities also inclines to make them musical.

They must avoid hesitancy in choice or action and not take on the problems of the whole world, lest other's misfortunes weigh too heavily on emotions to allow them to be of any help. Neither must they allow sensuality to take their strength.

They are domestic and parental by instinct, tending to enjoy both the life of the recluse and the social whirl, in turn. They make good managers, able to coordinate and consider all sides.

The name "Jericho," whose walls were broken down, meant "moon," and Cancer, too, has defensive walls like the shell of a crab. The rites of Cancer were anciently celebrated in Ephesus, where Diana was worshipped. Since silver is the metal sacred to the Moon, the silversmiths did a good business there in forming objects of worship—until Paul came along.

The Cancerian must not react too sensitively to outer stimuli, neither let emotions become intensely concentrated, lest their activity be held within the environmental shell and directed unhealthily inward. He must extend himself beyond the limits of his shell to let things out.

The astral world is the region of the soul's desires, plastic and movable. Like the ocean, it has a restless yet insistent quality. It is a sea of sensations or emotions. The Cancerian has psychic-etheric "feelers," which he projects as antennae to touch and gather impressions of people and places. Through this feeler-force, he quite accurately judges the reactions and thoughts of other people.

He has thus incarnated in order to learn life-lessons through experiences with home and family affairs. In business, he might incline to one of small profit and quick turnover, with popular appeal. He likes "the people" in a parental sort of way.

Intense sensitivity wakens inner impressions both to the seen and the unseen, but contact with the world in general sometimes causes inhibitive reactions, where he withdraws from unpleasantness. He has an active and fruitful imagination, which must be positively directed.

In Cancer occurs the "leap" from one generation to the next, and from one spiral of evolution to another, as one rises into the spiritual worlds.

Fourth House — Color: Orange-yellow
"I go to prepare a place for you..."

Here is the Root of existence and the *place* of personal establishment, environment and location. This is home base, the base of operations, and place of refuge or shelter, the Estate.

It rules parents (usually the mother or less aggressive parent when young; both parents when one has grown), genealogy, ancestry or family Tree. It rules both gestation and the latter part of life on earth.

It is the place of the Incubation of life and of the nourishment thereof. This involves food and protection.

This house deals also with changes of residence; lands, mines, and agriculture; real estate.

LEO

(Approximately July 23 – August 23)
Fifth Sign – Ruled by Sun

At 120 degrees from the beginning point of the Zodiac its first trine is completed and we enter Fixed-Fire sign **Leo**, where the initial Creative Fire of Aries is channeled into a more stabilized form so that its vital forces may be organized and controlled. This area is called the Mansion of Power and Glory, where reside Focalized Fire and the solar radiation of Spirit.

In Leo, man goes beyond the Arian's first discovery of himself, and seeks to know himself better so that he might consolidate this knowledge of what he really is into a better expression of Self-radiating joy and love. This area refers to the early development of the love and desire nature along with consciousness of self in relation to soul and form.

This sign carries the Principle of Cosmic Splendor with the inherent magnificence of the sun—not that the sun's rulership makes Leo more important than other signs but its energies resemble solar power, radiating an attractive personal warmth which at best draws others into a circle about them.

At the time Leo was named, the sun, at the celestial apex of its power and glory, was entering the sign a month earlier than is now the case. This radiant power of the sun, descending through the lunar forces of Cancer, brings Life and form to Matter. After the form has been ensouled and gently nourished by the moon, the sun leaves the womb to spring forth in all its splendor and to take on vital physical life, and by its full heat to mature and ripen the grain for Virgo's reaping.

On close inspection, the glyph drawn for Leo may be seen as an inside-out Cancer symbol—the semi-circles which once faced inward to nurture have now been "extroverted," the Son having been born. The two halves of the symbol, which were before separated, are now joined into one, establishing a link between the inner soul of man and the power of the Sun above, so that the solar energy may freely circulate its flow of Life through the sons of man.

The symbol for this sign is in appearance reminiscent of the human heart with its two valves a center of the human circulatory system. The areas of the physical body ruled by Leo are the heart and aorta, the circulation of the blood, the sides and back, and the spine and vital fluid.

Leo means "Lion." Yet another suggestion for this symbol is that of the mane of a lion whose air of kingly authority is not unlike that of a Leo native. The force of the lion is sometimes likened to the serpent power, or Kundalini, another name for the spinal fire which is shown here in its latent aspect, where it must wait until the being has become sufficiently evolved to handle it, for it can be dangerous uncontrolled, but when restrained it becomes a source of power.

The Leo person usually has the regal bearing and impressive manner of the King of Beasts for which he is named, along with a dignified sense of worth, courage and fairness which make him capable as a leader or ruler, and help to win respect.

He is direct in speech and because of intense feeling may express somewhat dramatically. He is usually trusting and trustworthy and this faith in his fellow beings is one of his secrets of success. He is inclined to be generous and is not "small" or mean. He may react with righteous indignation at any affront to his sense of values.

As ruler of the heart, his nature is warmhearted and affectionate and his personal development requires both the giving and receiving of love. The Leo child especially has a need for love, in order to grow wholesomely. "Love is the fulfillment of the law." Yet he must learn to rule his own heart wisely. Children respond to his spontaneous warmth and he usually loves them.

Ruled by the Sun (Son), this is the sign of the Child and of all things pertaining to children, such as schools and teaching. It refers to all personal creations both of body and of mind (such as art), being the sign of the Life-giving orb.

The less-evolved being may mistake pleasures or amusements for real joy and follow these shallow substitutes in a merry whirl of parties, theatre, gambling, luxuries and adornments. But he must learn to discern that outer show and ostentation are not the real thing and he must learn not to become deluded into vainglorious attitudes or vulgar pretenses.

Despite the inner assurance of grandeur, he must also learn the value of humility in finding true happiness and balance. He prefers to be the magnanimous giver, but he must not be too proud to accept sincerely-offered help or gifts of others at certain times. His is the ability to command or govern and he must use this leadership ability for the good of others, not to satisfy the ego's desire for earthly kingship or domination.

Leo is a hot, dry, Fixed-Fire sign. The temples of Apollo are dedicated to the life-giving rays of the Sun, as the Psalms of David are songs of love lifted up in praise to God. The rites of Leo were anciently celebrated by the Greeks in their revels honoring Dionysus and Bacchus. Sun-worship was known to many nations.

In some of their ceremonies Egyptian priests wore the skins of lions to symbolize the solar orb, which rules Leo and is considered fortunately placed therein.

Fifth House — Yellow on the Color Wheel
"Except ye become as a little child..."

This is the joyous sector devoted to personal warmth and affection, the heart's love of others in its circle, especially in relation to romance and courtship, or of children. It refers both to creation and recreation of all kinds.

The fifth house relates to all schools and teaching, below college level at least. It refers to children in general, as well as to those works 'begotten" through artistic endeavor.

Relegated here are all types of fun and recreation, whether theatre or sports, and the dress and adornment which pride or good taste dictate to make one attractive to loved ones or an admiring public.

In this house are shown the condition of the "heart" and the "backbone," both physically and psychologically.

VIRGO

(Approximately August 23 – September 23)
Sixth Sign – Ruled by Mercury

The essence of **Virgo** rests in its urge toward efficiency and perfection. There is an element of idealism, of ever seeking to find that which is perfect in the world of form and finding it needful to correct or reject that which does not measure up.

As the Principle of Cosmic Perfection and of usefulness, he emphasizes the truth that all things are on the way toward perfection. He heralds a Golden or Edenic Age which knows Service and the conscientious devotion to duty as a privilege.

The pictograph of the Virgin carrying a sheaf of grain signifies the state of ripeness which is the perfection of Nature in both animal and vegetable kingdoms. The letter M as a basis of the Virgo symbol has attached at its end the Phoenician symbol for a fish. Early Christians also used the fish as a clue to the mystery of the virgin birth. Having gathered the ripened grain, she stands pure and unspoiled at the brink of Libra, or the fulfillment of her role.

Virginal purity and dedication are needed to bring about the birth of the Messiah in the vehicle of the Cosmic Man. Only purified matter can merge with the Christ; thus, Purity becomes its first concern. Without ulterior or selfish motive was the Fiat of unquestioning readiness to accept Divine mandate given by the Wise Virgin Mary.

The non-animal symbol of Virgo comes as the teacher of the Immaculate Conception. This purity is not necessarily celibacy in the spiritual aspirant, but purity of intent, thought, and feeling. Selfish desire is not pure. The *M* of the Virgo symbol in contrast with that of Scorpio shows a closing-over of the female generative organs, the Scorpio *M* with its upturned arrow indicates the generative power in action.

The Sphinx is said to combine the aspects of the Leo Lion with the Virgo maiden, thus symbolizing union of Spirit and matter. The Life-giving rays of Solar vitality join the field of earth and matter to bring fruitfulness into perfection through the overshadowing of the Lord of Hosts. This increase is the emblem of the harvest season, traditionally in September.

Virgo is the mutable Earth sign, cold, feminine and dry. In ancient tradition, a Virgin goddess at this season visited the Planet Earth to teach mankind the arts of agriculture and fruitfulness. She became their goddess of harvest.

In Peru, an ancient festival was dedicated to Virgo at which time special honor was shown to women. In India, Virgo is known as "Durga," and considered a goddess of dignity and power. Ancient rites of Virgo were celebrated in the Eleusinian Mysteries at Attica. Christian rituals also relate the Virgin Mary to the sign Virgo, celebrating her nativity or birthday on September 8.

Vulcan, the little-known planet so close to the Sun as to be invisible to us, is sometimes called the ruler of Virgo. Mythologically, he was a blacksmith or metalworker and the god of Fire. But for practical purposes, the planet Mercury, also very near the Sun, is the one actually used as Virgo's ruler.

This is a different aspect of Mercury from that of Gemini, for it tends to sort out the ideals which Gemini so profusely gathered. Hence the thorough precision of Virgoan's methods. Devoted to minute detail and the sectioning of ideas and thoughts, they must not lose perspective of the whole in their attention to the parts. They tend to be more constructive than creative. The square aspect to Gemini 90 degrees away indicates the intelligence through which self-consciousness came about.

The digestive system is ruled by Virgo, that upper area of the intestinal tract where the usable elements of food are sorted out and dispatched to various parts of the body and the refuse discarded. It is a process of separating and assimilating in order to incorporate only the pure essences.

In harmony with this is another trait of this sign—that is health, cleanliness and hygiene. For this reason, it produces proficient nurses and dietitians, and sometimes persons who keep their home rather sterile with neatness. They can be very adaptable and practical companions, however, and the sign also refers to such homely, earthy things as gardens, orchards and small animals, which they tend to enjoy.

The Virgoan may correct verbally the imperfections he sees in the actions of others and may be thought petty for pronounced attention to detail. He may become skeptical in tending to believe only what is outwardly manifest, but his analytical tendencies extend as much to himself as to others; so, he may become quite self-critical. He makes an excellent professional critic.

He must learn correct discrimination, to know the false from the real and to appraise aright, so that any adjustment may be a wholesome one. He must avoid wasting vital energies, having no flow-through direct aspect from the fiery beginning in Aries; but this state of comparative neutrality endows him with a sort of happy innocence, almost a naivete.

Service is his mainstay in working to help others, and he can be happily busy in simple things. A loyally devoted and efficient employee, he is most dependable and thorough. In God's most humble servant, mind and hand work together to produce results, whether he be priest, office worker or laborer.

Only through the Ideal of Service does man truly grow beyond the primary state of education begun with the Child in Leo.

Virgo represents the maturing of personality still young and unspoiled, with the soul lifted up to areas of higher awareness.

But one gift do I ask
This is service with a task
Never ending until the time
When I leave this earthly vehicle behind.
Then to rest and start anew
To help some others that have but few
Of those precious gifts Thou givest Me,
Love, Wisdom, and Charity!

❧

Sixth House — Color: Yellow-green
"I have no will but to do the Will of Him that sent me..."

This area shows dedication to duties with true appreciation of the value of service. There is a readiness to work and to perform willing labor, as well as the projection of an attitude of good-neighborliness and helpfulness. Ideally, this is both the renunciate and the perfectionist in Service.

If employed by others, the employee-potential of the individual is shown in this house, otherwise that of those whom he employs. Other things depicted by Virgo are armed services, labor unions; health, digestion and hygiene; health foods; faculties of critical analysis; and small animals and gardens.

LIBRA

(Approximately September 23 – October 23)
Seventh Sign – Ruled by Venus

Libra weighs the grain which Virgo reaps. Having learned consideration of others through service in Virgo, man comes now to the point of full maturity, where he is willing to recognize the worthiness of another to share with him on equal terms both life and goods, and the search for happiness. In this way the personal self becomes selfless, having attained its full development in the area of form; now his only need is for spiritual growth, or learning to function with the soul for self-expansion.

This brings out Libra's relationship to marriage, partnership and the "other fellow" in general—whoever stands on an equal footing with the individual concerned. This also relates to any kind of opponents or opposition.

In Libra is depicted the Cosmic Principle of Mutuality, in which all things are seen to have mutual relationships and reciprocal rights. The power of this sign is that of fusion through uniting, the development of human relationships to a fine art.

The True Marriage is the divine one of the lower self to the Higher, which takes place at the time of God-Realization. Earthly marriage is but a shadow of the heavenly patterns, wherein the energy of solar radiation unites with substance in order to sustain and stimulate the life of form.

The Libran has a pronounced urge to unite with others or to relate to them harmoniously. His desire for equality and reciprocity can best be expressed through marriage which means much to this natural "helpmeet." To him loving and being loved, and doing things together, are important. His idea of love is that of a force which achieves perfect balance or equipoise between two equal, but unlike, forces in mutual support of each other.

The word *Libra* means "balance" or "scales." The entrance of the sun into this sign marks the beginning of autumn and the fall equinox ("equal night and day"), as the sun crosses the celestial equator midway between longest day and longest night of the solstices and brings about a state of balance between sun and earth for this day.

After the activities of spring and summer, the tree sap returns to the roots and nature's life-forces draw back within once more. The sun, in the sign opposite its exaltation in Aries, is said to be at its 'fall" in Libra.

This sign is to the year as sunset is to the day, the time of laying down tools, weighing the harvest and going into the "other half' of life and experience. This is the opportunity to expand personal horizons through seeking out companionship or social life, or to spend time pursuing mental, cultural or artistic activities.

In the "evening" of personal life and the rounding-out of self-application, man faces his alter-ego across the span of his horizon, and through other people is able to re-evaluate himself, as though filling the other pan of the scales.

The symbol drawn to represent Libra is somewhat like the setting sun, as it sinks below the horizon—the one half seen, the other unseen—or again, it appears like the two dissimilar halves of one unit, as in marriage. But even more appropriately, it seems to represent the beam of the scales from which are suspended the two balance pans—the beam representing Will and the two pans, which must reach equal poise, representing the head and the heart, or thought and feeling, as one learns to reorganize the difference between Self and not-Self.

It is the perfect equilibrium of the inner and outer, which permits true health and harmony. Thus, there is a need for one continually to weigh himself and his life situations in order to determine correctly what ingredients are needed to strike the proper balance and to consider carefully before making decisions regarding both people and things.

The goddess of Justice is always shown holding scales in which to weigh evidence of what is known and seen in order to correctly determine the values of the unseen, so as to mete out fair judgment. The Libran individual has a fine sense of justice and thinks of all men as equal. He is keenly perceptive, with the insight to assess situations and impartially appraise people. His powers of cognition and impersonal comparison make him an excellent judge. He does not incline, like Gemini, to choose between two possibilities, but to try to unite the two in harmony together and use both.

In mythology, Athena and Astrea were called the patrons of the codes of justice and law, designed to protect the rights of people to live in peace and harmony. Athena was also known as the goddess of wisdom, in view of the fact that Libra is one of the air or mental signs. The scales are the only inanimate object used to symbolize a sign of the zodiac, for then the personal aspect is removed that the justice might be totally unbiased.

The pope wears the hieroglyph of Libra as one of his chief ornaments.

Being the cardinal, or active sign of mind, Libra makes for independent thinking, receiving through its trine aspect to Gemini the influence of Divine Intellection. Its opposition aspect to Aries shows separation from the Sun-Father, while Saturn's exaltation in Libra shows the earth-father influence. The square of this sign to Cancer is suggestive of a break from the instinctual Oversoul, making a fresh start or turning a corner, as is the case with every square. The reaction or opposite result of Aries' action is the stimulation of mind into activity. Librans are mentally active, communicative and expressive, with definite tendencies toward mental enterprise.

Adam and Eve were driven from Eden after tasting the apple, later called sacred to Venus, the goddess of love and ruler of Libra. Her rulership brings out the aspect of beauty, and the cultivation of refinement in order to surpass Nature's endowments, as in the arts, literature and the social graces. All these add to the beauty of things beyond the mere necessity of their function. The giving of himself to others creates spiritual beauty in him who gives, as well as in the situation or relationship itself.

On the negative side, Libran persons may be indecisive, weighing things too long in their minds. They may tend to seek out others in order to find the balance for qualities lacking in themselves, and must avoid attaching themselves to others for moral or physical support. They must learn independence.

Libra, as the cardinal or leading air sign, is also considered a hot, moist, semi-fruitful sign; it is called a human, scientific, positive and masculine sign. Physically it rules the venous blood circulation, kidneys and loins.

On Venus' day, Friday, Jesus shed his blood. As the seventh sign and that of Saturn's exaltation, there is some suggestion of affinity with the Sabbath.

❧

Seventh House — Green on the Color Wheel
"What God therefore hath joined together..."

The extension of the first-house "I" to its opposite extreme becomes "thou," in the sense of the other person or persons with whom one must deal on a basis of equality. This refers both to those who cooperate as partners of marriage, business or circumstance, and to those who oppose as open enemies, or rivals, in any field. It refers to the other team in sports, and to the other country in war. The worthy opponent.

Mutuality in general is of this house, the attempt to maintain harmony and peace in order to balance the scales of relationships. The person with many planets in the seventh house may find many relationships with people, and the need to learn cooperation, adaptation, and deference to the ways of others.

This is called the house of marriage, of your counterpart or mate, as well as of the client, if you work in an advisory capacity, and of the public in general. Cultural tastes and social tendencies are shown here.

Scorpio

(Approximately October 23 – November 22)
Eighth Sign – Ruled by Pluto

*"Those who wait on the Lord shall renew their
strength, and shall mount up with wings as eagles."*

Scorpio represents the active Principle of Cosmic Purpose or Intention which shapes and prepares all things toward a definite end. Man's prerogative of free will in the cultivation of Self demands much self-discipline, and Scorpio is a sign capable of voluntary training due to his strength of determination and will.

His rich intensity of feeling and thought seem to surge up from some inner depth to find expression in a most compelling way. His powerhouse of emotional energy must be firmly controlled and directed into channels for constructive, rather than destructive, use.

As ruler of the sexual function, Scorpio relates to all forms of growth, for through this most intimate and mystical process we are each transformed from a single cell into a human being. The soul within deeply remembers its patterns of life-experience when it did occupy but one tiny cell; and even more distantly it remembers the experience of death, which it has known many times and must someday face again. Scorpio seems to have a basic urge to re-identify with the Source from whence it came.

November's cold and sometimes dreary weather in this northern hemisphere heralds the time to go within-doors and make use of inner resources in the darker winter months. Yet this was the favorite sign of the old alchemists who considered Scorpio the most fertile time to accomplish their works.

It is called a fruitful, feminine, negative and reproductive sign—the Fixed Water sign. A material form of fixed water is ice, as substance easily melted by heat. Scorpio has to do with bodies of still, deep water, as well as with swamps or stagnant water, and even with sewage and sanitation.

In philosophy, fixed water represents stabilized and intensified emotions, as well as solidified impressions imprinted upon the soul or subconscious mind. It is the emotional energy which was set into motion in the first water sign, Cancer, and has now deepened and strengthened into this intense force of creative desire, a fixed power in the process of being charged and transmuted.

Through Mars' co-rulership of this sign, "red" water may be said to relate to the Red Sea, which parted to let God's children pass safely through.

Having no favorable aspect to the Primal Triad of the first three signs and being in square aspect to Life-giving Leo, Scorpio has come to be called the sign of death and of the Old Testament curses which followed Adam and Even from Eden, from whence they were banished with shame and pain into darkness and the assurance of death because of their rebellion. This death is not only *from* physical life but also *into* physical life.

Scorpio's trine aspect to protective Cancer saves him from complete death. For though he is separated from his Source on this battlefield of the Soul, he can always bridge the abyss by remembering God and aspiring to Him with his whole being. As the fourth sign, Cancer indicates the place one occupies; so, the double-four, or eighth sign, Scorpio, relates to another but physically unseen place through which the soul must pass, beyond the mysterious portal called death. This same door symbolizes the passageway one attempts to enter in the studies of the "hidden" or occult sciences.

The symbol for Scorpio depicts the female generative organs, barbed with a cupid's dart to show the lure of the senses. It also resembles a scorpion, the creature which depicts the lower stage of Scorpio's evolution. Its dwelling place in the shadows and the venomous and death-dealing sting in its tail make this, in its unevolved aspect, a symbol to be feared. The tongue of this person may at times lash out with a similar sting of biting sarcasm.

He feels an urge for self-expression and, while awaiting the attainment of the higher Self, he may use his strong will as a means of preparation to destroy or drive certain undesirable conditions from his life. This brings out Scorpio's relationship to the expulsion of waste or excrement, as the sign also ruling the eliminatory organs, or bladder and rectum.

Mayan Indians called Scorpio the sign of the death god. Elsewhere, it was represented as half scorpion and half man—the human half belonging to the upper regions, and the lower half to the underworld. The man was eventually replaced by the eagle as a symbol of that power in man which is able to rise above the temptations of his primitive impulses.

An eagle, symbol of the transmutation of lower nature, is able to ascend from the ground and soar upward into the higher mental and spiritual realms. This king of birds is an ancient symbol of spiritual vision and is said to be the only creature that can look directly into the Sun. The Scorpio person tends to have penetrating vision, somewhat as an "eagle's eye."

The phoenix bird is an alternate symbol for regenerated Scorpio, this bird which tradition says rose alive from its own ashes. A less-used symbol for the highest aspect of this sign is the dove, as one who goes a step beyond even the level of eagle-consciousness to carry its message of love and bring an end to fear.

Scorpio is not the most easily understood of signs, for he is both outspoken and secretive, both violent and controlled. He may be brutal as a criminal, or tender and magnanimous with children.

The extremes of agony and ecstasy, of sex and death, are his lot. He either hates or loves intensely, all or nothing; he does not go half-way. He is a courageous soldier, sometimes a vindictive enemy, a loyal friend, or a fierce opponent; and the power of his convictions may make him willing to die for any cause of which he is champion. Yet he hesitates to give full expression to his feelings because of their depth, but rather tends to take experiences within himself. This strong silence makes him seem the more powerful and magnetic, and a fine father-confessor."

His lust for life experiences may get him into trouble. He may doubt existent codes of justice, and rebelliously attempt to take the law into his own hands. He can be violent in passion, whether jealousy, anger or lust, yet is more capable than most of icy self-control, as seen for example by his typically powerful work as a surgeon, a healer, or a secret agent. His passionate intensity is excellent for scientific research and investigation of things hidden, whether in occult or worldly fields.

Whereas Libra's rule over the internal generative organs adds to the Venusian attraction toward sharing life with another, Scorpio's rulership of the external generative organs carries forth into Mars-action the expulsion of life-seeds so that another generation may carry on where it leaves off. Mars deals with the creative power through sex, whereas Pluto's rulership over the underworld brings about the relation of the sign to death. In both appears an aspect of jumping from one life-stage to another.

The serpent of Eden represented man's sexual power descended like the fallen angel Lucifer to a baser level of self-gratification, where it controlled man and he was unable to refuse it. In misuse of this power, man destroys life and himself in the dying embers of the Divine Creative Fire. It is only when he tires of savagery and the dregs of existence and feels distaste as did the Prodigal Son among the swine, that he can at last fully turn this physical fervor into the spiritual ecstasy of the mystic in his triumph over the fallen Lucifer who once tripped him up.

This does not require celibacy even in priesthood. It requires lifting up the sexual energies through gaining perfect control over them—not letting them run you. It also demands that man regain proper respect for this great creative function in which one cooperates with God to bring forth life—or in which he shares with his mate a transcendent and beautiful experience of unity. Don't take it and hide it away from God, but share it with Him. Don't cover it with smutty implications, but remove the ugly layer of man's misapplication and restore it to its rightful place in God's plan.

When emotional energy has been transformed, it becomes a tremendous power for good; and when desire is transmuted, but not destroyed, its force helps supply the motive power for spiritual accomplishment. Scorpio represents that span of man's life when he is under threat of the "fall." It is also the place of regeneration, where the second birth is prepared and the veil of the inner temple is rent.

Eighth House — Color: Green-blue
"Except I be lifted up..."

This house refers to the extension beyond the realm of personal ownership (as shown by the second house), into its opposite house, the eighth, where is seen the potential of shared ownership or gain through others, as opposed to personal earnings. This includes financial status of one's partner, as well as inheritance, gifts and bequests.

As related both to sex and death, it involves the passageway through the door between life and death or between the ordinary and the unknown. As such it refers also to occult studies in which one seeks to open doors into other realms beyond one's own, the ending of a cycle and the octave of eight.

It also refers to the powers of generation and regeneration; both death and rebirth; the seed and fermentation of life-germs. It represents the end of a span of life-day, where one enters a place called "mysterious" because it is not physically seen.

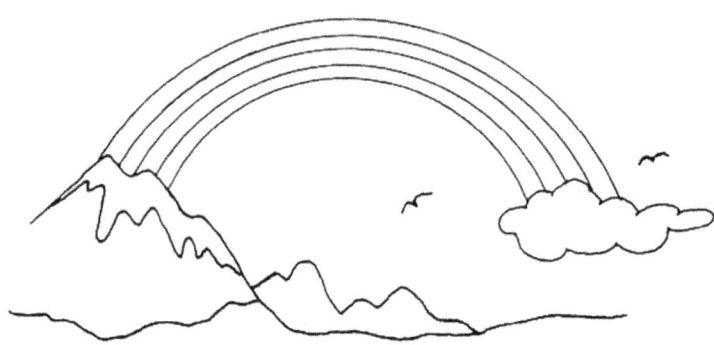

SAGITTARIUS
(Approximately November 22 to December 22)
Ninth Sign – Ruled by Jupiter

Mutable **Sagittarius** is the third sign of the Fire Triad. The first of these three, "Father Aries," now beckons to his son from afar to call him forth out of Scorpio's Egypt; and the son emerges from the land of temptation joyful and free. He has energy and driving power like Aries and the spirit-fed vitality of Leo, but lacks Aries' one-pointedness and Leo's open geniality. In square aspect to Virgo, Sagittarius has turned a corner to break away from Virgo's tidiness of pure form or matter to manifest more profusely, although less distinctly.

In opposition to Gemini, it carries that sign's aptitude for gathering information but past the personal and into the broader realms, seeking to expand its concepts in more abstract areas of inspired mind—as in religion and philosophy.

Called the Principle of Cosmic Progress, Sagittarius brings out the idea of ever-unfolding evolvement unto higher levels. It is interested in the Science of Law rather than in administration of justice and is quick in understanding the abstract ideas or principles behind things.

The unique cross in the glyph of Sagittarius is reminiscent of the veil having been rent in Scorpio and now moves forward into those higher realms it learned of there. The pictograph shows a centaur aiming an arrow. The word *sagitta* means "arrow" and *Sagittarius* means literally "archer." Traditionally, Sagittarius represented an archer shooting the Scorpion which had bitten Orion, another mighty star-hunter. Others said he was a wonderful Greek archer called Chiron who taught young people the skillful use of bow and arrow. The actual symbol for this sign shows a bowstring with an arrow being aimed upward with aspiration as though trying to pierce the skies. In storming heaven's gates, he seeks to translate its light into prophetic vision of religious philosophy.

As a dual creature combining the attributes of both horse and man, if there is conflict between the animal nature and the intellectual or spiritual ideals, he may tend to settle for one or the other. Spirit and flesh may have to strive for dominion, and if the lower half wins, he may spend his time at sports or restless roving, insisting on unrestrained "freedom." With his bow and arrow, he may become a hunter for food, sport, or revenge, or for trophies such as medals, cups, political plums, riches and seats of honor. If he drops the "animal" of his nature entirely he may be like the absent-minded professor—too detached from the natural world.

But, if his nature is in perfect harmony, he conjoins the two parts of his nature into one whole, as one who can enjoy physical exercise and outdoor life and keep his body in good shape while at the same time lifting his consciousness up unto the spiritual. He still works as man in the outer world, but with Spirit ever urging him higher; his upward aim must eventually lead him to the goal he envisions as consciousness expands to accept it. In aiming toward divinity, he transmutes or gradually leaves his animal body to identify with the human. The arrow also shows his enthusiasm of spreading new thoughts as an ambassador of ideas. Because of his seeking after mental expansion his wisdom may be sought and heard on subjects of science, philosophy, religion and travel to far places.

Another supposed meaning of the symbol is that it depicts the thighbones of the human body above the knee, joined together for single motivation, or for the forward "thrust" of the body. This brings out Sagittarius' rulership over the upper part of the legs— that which impels motion and aids the body in traveling. The thighs indicate the point of juncture of the legs, with the rest of the body, or the idea of the whole, being involved in movement.

Movement implies travel beyond one's immediate scope, especially as wide forays into the world of thought and ideas. Sagittarius likes adventuring into new realms of mind and place, to explore the world and to try new projects. He deals with the scope and breadth of adventure and opportunity, as well as of geographical exploration into outer territories. Travel is indicated, both of mind and body, with broadening concepts of worship and upliftment of consciousness. His interest is to express freedom and explore extensively beyond the natural or known environment. He is idealistic, free-ranging and far-reaching in his ambition for "propulsion into space," like his arrow in search of freedom. One reason for the scope of Sagittarius is given by astronomers who say that in the extreme reaches of space, far beyond the seen constellation of Sagittarius and behind a thick, impenetrable cloud of bright stars, lies the great Central Sun around which our own solar system moves.

Sagittarius is said to be "ruled" by the planet Jupiter because its nature is similar to that of the jovial planet which is largest in our solar system and is therefore related to the idea of largesse and expansion. The Principle of Cosmic Abundance is associated with Sagittarius and Jupiter is the expansive growth principle in all form. Jupiter is benevolent and philanthropic, offering of his material substance to fill the great need of others. He is inclined to be "well off," if a member of the so-called "middle class," comfortable, affable and generous. He knows that potentially there is plenty of good supply for all people, and acts accordingly. His optimistic nature sees the positive side of things.

For himself, he seeks abundance of mental material for expansion and his generous nature opens to the dawning of larger conceptions. Those more enlightened who are under its influence seem to function with Neptune as well, in more nebulous fields of liberation or preservation of the general good.

Sagittarius as a mutable or common Fire Sign is considered positive, hot, dry, masculine, flexed and double-bodied. In the physical body, it rules the hips and thighs, sciatic nerve, arterial blood, liver and the two adrenal glands which are productive of poise.

Some Sagittarian attributes of both positive and negative nature are: foresight and prophecy—or spiritual/mental flightiness; swiftness of motion related to the movement of an arrow through space—or love of speed and swift sports, athletics, horse-racing and fast cars. While an excellent companion of positive outlook and refreshing cheer, he can be unnecessarily frank and outspoken with something of humorous sarcasm. He cares little for listening, preferring to anticipate what he thinks the other may have in mind. He may enjoy argument as an exercise of wit. He lacks precision and punctuality, tending to disregard time and space.

While generous, he can turn to wastefulness if negatively oriented. While jovial, he may become over-optimistic and spoiled with indulgence. He may have good political or social "connections" through lodge or church to help someone out of a jam, or may use these things to further his own interests and position. He should not exaggerate the importance of "position," nor feel overly impelled to be part of an "in" group.

His sense of adventure and love of novelty makes him seek a variety of experience, but may also make him seem inconstant. He must keep his aim high to avoid foolishly wasting his life in mere lust for pointless adventure.

Ancient religious rites of Sagittarius were the Mysteries of the Centaurs, featuring Chiron, the teacher of Achilles. These rites originated in Atlantis. Poseidon, or Neptune, was also patron of the horse.

❧

Ninth House — Blue on the Color Wheel
"Set your hope on those things which are above..."

The ninth house rules philosophy and religion, and the mind up-reaching into all abstract or higher realms of thought. As opposite the mental third house, the intellect extends its aim in a search for higher learning, and aspires to progress.

Here we take long journeys either in body or thought, in travel or any dealings with foreign lands or peoples. Here too is the "broadcasting" of the knowledge gathered in the third house, with greater scope, breadth, and the benevolence of expansion and largesse.

In ancient times, religion tended more toward philosophy than theology, and the temples were also universities.

Confucius said, "In order to know man, one may not dispense with a knowledge of heaven."

Man is unconsciously motivated by his time/space origins to seek recognition of some pattern to his life, in the symbols of the universe of nature outside himself—to relate the details of his Being to the all-embracing Cosmic-Patterns.

A clear insight into the essential need for religion is gained by one who becomes aware of the beautifully-created designs within which our lives are regulated, and which ultimately balance and justify all.

CAPRICORN
(Approximately December 22 – January 20)
Tenth Sign – Ruled by Saturn

*"Who shall ascend the hill of the Lord? And who shall stand in
this holy place? He who has clean hands and a pure heart..."*

Capricorn is the sign at the zenith of the horoscope, elevated
to the very top of the wheel. Obviously, it represents the height
of worldly endeavor, the position sought after, one's prominence or
standing in the public eye. It shows the purpose or direction of human
efforts, as well as that which has control over the activities. As the
highest point the soul can reach in this round of incarnation, it has
to do with the high seats of government and authority. It is a place of
power and responsibility.

Spiritually, it represents the Presence of the Most High, and the
Orders of the Hierarchy or governing body of the heavens, along
with the laws which govern Creation. It represents Cosmic Order and
Justice, with appreciation of the hierarchical ideal, of various levels of
authority and respect for the worthy. The sign chosen to govern and
control becomes the father image of mankind. In order to prove his
worth in holding these positions of trust, he must face and overcome
difficult obstacles, be tried and tested, and sometimes persecuted and
misunderstood. In this he gains a profound depth and unsurpassed
sincerity. He keeps silent about his suffering, and uncomplainingly
accepts responsibility.

Capricorn is the leading or cardinal Earth Sign, thus an active expression of earthly, practical attributes. In the human anatomy, it rules the knees, the skeleton and bones or joints, the teeth, gall bladder, and skin—pretty much the framework and physical boundary of the human body.

The symbol drawn to represent Capricorn is variously described. One explanation is that it was to show the human knee, and that all zodiacal symbols were meant to depict the part of the anatomy which they represent. This is justified by saying the knee is that which enables man to stand in upright position and to climb (as well as to kneel).

A more usual explanation of the symbol is that it depicts the mountain goat with a curled fish's tail, or again the horns of a mountain goat—that fearless climber who insists on reaching to the highest and least accessible places of earth. The motive power of a goat is like the ambition which may drive a Capricorn person to the topmost crag of the physical world, or in some cases of the spiritual. At the same time, he can dip with his fish's tail into the depths of the subconscious mind and draw intuitively from its storehouse of memory. *Caper*—a goat, and *Cornu*—a horn.

Capricorn seeks to rise to perfection on all levels, from depths to heights. His caution and independence sustain him on his climb, gathering up riches of experience until reaching his own. It is, like Scorpio, a sign of extremes, yet of prudence and persistence. The double-five, which adds to ten of the tenth sign, shows the dual nature of Man whose number is five—or man plus his shadow, doubling five. If he goes beyond to attain spirituality, he becomes man plus his Light in Christ.

Another symbol of Capricorn is the unicorn, a creature victorious in all tests, and mythical enemy of the lion, which symbolizes the serpent power in man. The unicorn mobilizes into action the latent serpent power of Leo, and it is from the Saturn center in man that this power begins to rise.

In Greek mythology, this sign was correlated with the god Pan, ruler of things rural such as shepherds and woodlands, and called the god of Plenty. From this comes the cornucopia or horn of Plenty. Pan had a man's head but goat legs. He was also called Jupiter-Pan as a lord of the world. The generating power of the Sun was represented as a goat-man. The name of the dark pillar of King Solomon's temple is Boaz, which means "strength, as in a goat."

Certain mythical "culture gods" were said to come from the sea (of the subconscious mind) periodically to teach man the ways of civilization, returning to the sea each night. One such Fish-man was Oannes, a great being dressed in a tight fish-like suit who taught one of the ancient nations all things they needed to know.

Capricorn was a sign venerated by the ancients, a favorite among astrologers. It is, next to its opposite sign Cancer, the least conspicuous among the constellations. Whereas Cancer represents the door to physical birth, Capricorn is the door to spiritual birth and initiation; and as Cancer represents dwelling place and protective influence, Capricorn points to worldly or public position.

This animal sign is called the Cradle of Christ, as he was born among the animals in their manager or feeding trough. When the physical sun is at its point of lowest manifestation, its shortest day, the spiritual sun is born symbolically at the time of the winter solstice, when the sun enters Capricorn, called the "Southern Gate of the Sun."

Even as Scorpio had to sacrifice his mortal life for immortal Truth, Capricorn must sacrifice the lifeblood of his material substance to rise to spiritual heights. Materialism is shown by all earth signs, Capricorn being doubly linked to the physical through Saturn, and through Mars' exaltation in this sign. These are called the lords of the astral and physical realms. It is in Capricorn that these realms must be subjected, or put under control, before one may withdraw attention from the physical. The corporeal body must be mastered and made to serve man's will, as the perfection of the preceding earth sign Virgo should now manifest the perfection of the Virgin in the

70

objective world, in the perfect human order. The square aspect from Libra indicates struggle.

The key to Capricorn's success is patient perseverance. Contention with Matter is vanquished by the ordeal of patient labor. His inclination toward silence and taking things seriously help him to learn more, but may make him misunderstood, sometimes seem "old-fashioned." He takes responsibility seriously and his concern for the welfare of all may cause him to openly criticize or chastise. Capricorn's organizing ability fits him for executive positions. It is a sign of business, but he should be about his Father's business.

He insists on complete realization of his goal through serious work and earnest endeavor. On the lower level he turns to politics; on the higher level he makes a great statesman. The rulership of Saturn causes waiting, serious work, denial and discipline. Fear must be transmuted. Saturn is contractive, indicating concrete action. It can make man impervious to spirit, or bring its greatest light.

It represents crystallization through worldly involvement to cause material darkness, or seduction of the soul. When the spiritual being seeks oneness with God the Father to gain wise counsel, the Darkness must be lit by Christ-consciousness. He may be beguiled into literalism or the delusion that only what you see has valid existence. He may think of form as greater than spirit, or letter as greater than the idea that produced it. His cycle of evolution is dedicated to experience. As the leading Earth sign, it is dry, feminine, passive, restrained or delusions of formalism. Capricorn is enterprising and prudent, with ability to organize others and help them manifest their best. His rational attitude gives an urge to conform to disciplined behavior. He is critical but forgiving, generous but practical. This sign represents death of the lower mind and birth of the spiritual.

☙

Tenth House — Color: Indigo or Blue-violet
"What shall it profit a man if he shall gain the whole world and lose his own soul?" (Mark 8:36)

The extension of the fourth house straight up from "home base," reaches to the tenth, at the peak of worldly achievement, or the position of public honor which one establishes before others.

This is the mountain-top view of the world, the place of arrival at the goal of earthly attainment. It shows worldly eminence, or public position, business or profession, the career of one's choice. It can also show notoriety and fame. It represents governing bodies, whether of a city, nation, or world order, and indicates the authority which controls man's ends or which he thinks controls them.

"The pure practice of celestial philosophy in course of time became corrupted into the worship of the heavens and afterwards into idolatry, or the worship of images found to resemble certain qualities of the planets in honor of which they were instituted. At first, men began to attribute the effects, which they perceived were produced by the celestial bodies, to the powers of those bodies as gods or demons of an inferior rank to the great First Cause, whose majesty was gradually lost sight of to some extent."

AQUARIUS
(Approximately January 20 – February 19)
Eleventh Sign – Ruled by Uranus

"God is in this mountain, and through it and all around it, and He will dissolve it if you will let Him."

In the Mediterranean area, at the time when the signs of the Zodiac were named, the Sun's stay in what is now **Aquarius** coincided with the season of heavy rains, so it was natural to call the sign of this period the "water-bearer." It is also called Waterman, or Etheric Man; its ruler Uranus, meaning "heaven," indicates these to be heavenly waters. The Holy Grail is its symbol.

A great Celestial Sea was believed to occupy that area which released so much water to earth. The sign was anciently called Canopis, for the Egyptian water-god whose likeness appears on vessels used to keep the Nile waters in good drinking condition. He was considered the god who presided over the source of the river.

Early Christians associated Aquarius with John the Baptist. The action of water in baptism is said to effect a loosening of the etheric from the physical body. The cleansed and purified soul body takes on its pure white raiment as it comes into the glory of Christ-consciousness. It is in this etheric "water" that all the forces from the other signs are received, synthesized and balanced.

Not a "wet" earthly water, these are the Christ-ethers which carry spiritual and revitalizing power. Aquarius' rulership over the ethers and man's own etheric aura draws him into experience and vision on the etheric planes. To those whose consciousness is sufficiently raised, Christ will appear in this Age in an etheric body. The spiritual ideal of Aquarius is conscious cooperation with the Christos to further the evolution of the Cosmos.

The etheric sensitivity of Aquarius puts its natives more easily in touch with the Spirit of Truth, for Truth is said to be anchored in the etheric body, and is one of the key words of this sign. These people seem to know things without having to learn of them, things which may seem too simple to be true, even strange to those who demand literal explanation, but Time proves them out. They loyally stand by their convictions of Truth regardless of others' opinions, knowing these impressions inwardly received come from the more rarified level of Christ-ethers—to which they are sensitive—and such impressions are superior to earthly leads and worthy of obedience.

The Principle of Cosmic Solidarity is applied to this Fixed Air sign (moist, masculine, human, airy, intuitive and scientific). He brings about the fragrant flowering of perfected Man, and of mental maturity. In the fixation of the principle of Air, the Divine Breath which God breathed into Adam's earth-body has finally become solidly established there, and man becomes of Soul-age, perfected and complete in his attainment of function and able to use that breath himself to speak the Creative Word.

Man, now having conquered Matter, turns to the more inner work of spiritual realms, for in Aquarius matter and spirit become reconciled in man, where the two worlds meet. Full functioning in the brotherhood of Man on earth eventually leads to the great White Brotherhood where is given the chance to befriend man and function as a heavenly Big Brother.

Aquarius is the sign of friends. As the extension of Leo, or the sign furthest from and opposite Leo, the personal love has been carried forward and multiplied into less personal love for the many. The Aquarian is friendly and altruistic with humanitarian ideals, but less personally attached. Unlike Leo's awareness of self, he becomes aware of not-self, even to the point of self-denunciation. Carried to more extreme forms, this leads to lack of respect for human dignity or individual worth. It says that the individual counts as nothing beside the communal welfare of all. He sees himself equally small, so can call men his brothers, and willingly puts aside ego to give of self or share with others. This is being brought forth as a trend of the Aquarian Age. No one is a stranger to Aquarius. He likes to identify himself with progressive activities of the community.

Negatively, Aquarius can go into periodic silences or become silently angry. He is extremely independent and impatient of restraint and may show perverse or erratic behavior. He is unpredictable, unorthodox and, through detachment, can become unconventional. In extreme cases he may allow mistaken opinions to detract him from the Truth.

He is an independent and original thinker, progressive in thought as well as action. His reasoning intelligence blends with the faculty of intuition to further mental enlightenment. He puts his mental deductions to work in form as he tries out inventions or new methods— again, fixation of Air (mind).

The former ruler of Aquarius was Saturn—Time—but now it is Uranus—the "breaker of Time." Aquarius rules ankles, lower leg, central nervous system, ethers in body, body electricity and magnetic aura.

Its symbol of two horizontal lines in wavy or zig-zag form has been called several things. The first thought is rippling waves of water being poured from an urn, as a distillation of wisdom from knowledge being poured out for the benefit of all. ♒

All the air signs have dual lines. Here is a suggestion of air (wind) blowing over waters. Twin serpents have been mentioned; or the opposite polarities in electricity; or again, the conducting waves of light or electricity.

They are also said to depict the motion of one walking, raised up by the ankles with every step, since progress advances in waves, and there is a corresponding trough and crest with each wave. An apt meaning is vibratory energy, which dissolves all things back into a formless state by dissolution. This is its alchemical meaning.

Aquarius stands for unity in diversity. Joseph's coat-of-many-colors shows the Glory of God manifesting as man perfected through soul-transformation—converted into a Son of Man fit to receive the Son of God.

Greek myths identified the water-bearer as Ganymede, a beautiful shepherd lad chosen by Jupiter to act as cup-bearer for the Immortals and brought there on the back of an eagle. The rites of Aquarius pertain to the Mysteries of Ganymede who was also lord of the ethers, and keeper of the waters between heaven and earth.

Eleventh House — Violet on the Color Wheel
"And as ye would that men should do to you, do ye also to
them likewise." (Luke 6:31)

The urge toward love is extended from the smaller group of loved ones in the personal life (Fifth House) out into its opposite place on the circle, the impersonal expression of love toward the many; where no man is counted alien or strange, but all are part of one humanity, in the Eleventh House.

Friendship is a less personal form of love, and community activities in which the individual is subordinate to the group are akin to this house, as are all group activities.

Here also are hopes, wishes, and ideals. The solidification of thought deals with invention, ingenuity and the trying out of progressive ideas, as well as departure from convention.

The world brotherhood of Man below rises in potential even unto the White Brotherhood above.

PISCES
(Approximately February 19 – March 21)
Twelfth Sign – Ruled by Neptune

From Cosmic Grace or Forgiveness comes the virtue of charity. In self-offering **Pisces** desires to help the suffering, in this sign of renunciation where the hand of destiny is felt. Discipleship and devotion are his approach to the divine. He is capable of holiness through a sense of humility and sympathy, and can become a saint, mystic, or one who experiences the great sorrows.

In this twelfth and last sign of the Zodiac, the soul completes its cycle and retires in preparation for taking over a new vehicle, yet the circle never closes completely, for a spiral motion brings each round higher than the one before. Pisces has a strong link with the soul and can communicate between heaven and earth, spirit and substance.

The power of Pisces lies in the perfecting of man through his emotional nature. He sometimes lacks emotional control, allowing others to play on his sympathies to the point where he is torn between conflicting feelings. As third of the water or emotional signs, his feelings are neither obvious nor repressed like the others, but somewhat nurtured or brooded-over.

Neptune, which rules Pisces, was mythical god of the Deep, of the oceans and sea life. There is a mystery in that which lies beneath the waters, below the conscious level. The "waters" also refer to the psychic realm, so he may be very sensitive to other planes of consciousness, or somewhat mediumistic. He must avoid negative mediumship in which he would become subject to psychic control. The formlessness and boundlessness of oceans are suggested by his fluid nature, which is a bit difficult to "nail down" to particulars.

He tends to be misty or nebulous in thinking to escape into some vaporous depths and then emerge with impressions gained through intuition or contacts with other planes. Jupiter was called ruler of Pisces before the discovery of Neptune, and adds its expansive and outspreading inclination.

Water is the universal solvent, that which reduces all things to their primordial form (the "chaos" of the "great Unmanifest") breaking down all barriers. There is an innate desire to transcend material boundaries and a yearning for that which lies beyond. Pisces soulfully seeks to experience Simplicity of Being.

His tendency toward haziness leads to a relaxed attitude which finds difficulty in conforming to discipline or patterned forms of behavior. He likes to share in the emotion of others, but prefers to remain unbound by them. He tends to delude himself, thinking he can "charge it," enjoy now and pay later in life's situations, or foolishly imagines he can escape the laws of cause and effect. He may become carelessly easy-going, even shiftless, imprudent, or without purpose. Feeling out-of-element in the material world, he may evade responsibility or drift into a lazy world of dreams.

He must avoid self-pity, over-sensitivity, and wallowing in depressive thoughts or memories. He must avoid becoming the emotional parasite which attaches itself mercilessly to some object of affection to the point of near-suffocation; yet neither must he hurt loved ones with cruel disregard.

He may be led to plumb the depth of the ocean of sensuality, or seek escape in self-persecution, or in self-destructive habits, as drugs or alcohol, which also come under this sign. The rulership of Neptune over sleep and dreams inclines them to seek an artificial dream world, or liberation from material existence through those things which glamorize or make unreal that which can bring forth a poet, a musician, a fascinating romantic, or one dedicated to serving mankind in self-forgetfulness.

The idea of sleep implies retirement from action on the physical plane, and liberation into other realms. It is an area of retirement from the usual scenes of intense activity to places less seen, as in monasteries or institutions of any kind. One may either live or work in such a place. Placed here is such work as photography, radio, television, movies, or any other work done behind-scenes (or we might say, behind "seens") where the product is more evident than the worker—especially such work as involves illusion or glamour, as in the photographic arts.

Neptune has to do with spirituality, the mystic, the interpreter of things spiritual to the rest of humanity, universal love, and the selfless characteristics of Jesus, whose birth heralded the Age of Pisces. Venus, the goddess born of sea foam, is exalted in Pisces and lends her romantic charm.

Pisces is the Mutable Water sign, flexible, moist, cold, feminine, fruitful, negative, and psychic—a sign of expanded service. In the human being, it rules the feet, protoplasm, superphysical faculties, telepathy, and the chakras—also to a lesser extent, the nerve fibers and spinal cords.

As ruler of the feet, it helps man reach from place to place. The feet sustain the weight of the whole body in its contact with earth, and they also correlate with man's understanding. The symbol itself is sometimes said to depict two feet, supposedly poised between two paths.

More often though, the symbol is likened to two fishes tied together with a cord, each pulling in an opposite direction, one attempting to swim upstream and the other downstream, significant of the Piscean tendency toward duality. The cord relates to telepathy, to undersea or psychic communication, the link that unravels the mystery of two opposite but complementary halves of experience—involution and evolution. Fishes are strong and lithe, at home in Life's great Sea, and able to hold their own. They are said to symbolize the fertile point in the auric egg, in the creation of the universe.

This symbol is sometimes said to represent two crescent moons, waxing and waning, which symbolizes the receptive-intuitive or soul aspects of man, linked by the horizontal line of the material world, with one part facing back, the other forward.

The two crescents have been likened to the two halves of Aries pulled apart and sacrificed, then loosely tied. Since Aries is a ram, not a lamb, the Lamb of Sacrifice is said to belong to that point on the circumference of the Wheel where Pisces ends and Aries begins. It is at this point which can be called either 30 degrees of Pisces or zero degrees of Aries (they are the same), that the vernal equinox occurs, and the sun crosses the equator at the beginning of Spring. From this point our years are measured, and the right ascension of all stars calculated.

Twelfth House — Color: Violet-red
"Bless them that persecute you..." (Romans 12:14)

Here is the place of inventory, closing out the gathered assets of soul, as the wheel revolves to its close of cycle.

This house refers to dissolving or dissolution, and retirement from activity-in-form.

There is a withdrawal from the world in one way or another, as in institution, monastery, or hospital. This may be in voluntary service, or involuntary confinement as in evening up some score. It has to do with the charitable and compassionate who work with these people. This house rules retirement from visible or outer activity, seclusion, sleep, visions and dreams; it deals with spirituality and renunciation and atonement.

Mystery and secrets also find their place here, undiscoverable as though hidden in an ocean; glamour and illusion, or delusion. It rules all behind-the-scenes efforts as photography, radio, movies, or detective work where results, not processes, are seen.

THE
LANGUAGE OF
SYMBOLISM

THE LANGUAGE OF SYMBOLISM

"The heavens declare the glory of God; and the firmament
sheweth His handiwork. Day unto day uttereth speech, and
night unto night sheweth knowledge. There is no speech nor
language where their voice is not heard. Yet their line goes out
through all the earth, and their words to the end of the world."
—Psalm 19

"*The Speech of the Stars*"—that is the literal meaning of the term "astrology," and as the Psalmist said, "There is no language where their voice is not heard," for their field is so vast as to encompass the universe.

What do they say? Their speech is in the patterns drawn by the planets, each of which moves like a stylus across the heavens, tracing its invisible geometrical lines among the distant stars and suns. By number their paths can be discerned, and by harmony of position the nature of their effects can be determined, even as a musician can look at a diagram of notes and chords on paper, and tell at once whether the notes when struck will sound high or low, harmonious or discordant.

Some planets agree well with the nature of the sign or the backdrop of the heavens against which they are placed. Certain angular positions, such as the square aspect where two planets are placed at right angles in the circle of space, for some reason brings stress in these two areas. The observations of scientists, philosophers, and shepherd-priests through the ages since man was created have resulted in a store of knowledge which pretty well defines and anticipates the effects of the planets on human life and worldly affairs, as they faithfully move along their well-ordered paths.

We on earth are affected by them through the angular or geometrical patterns they form between each other in relation to our planet, and to their path around the sun from the one fixed, yet progressively moving, point where the spring equinox occurs each year.

SYMBOLS USED IN ASTROLOGY

A symbol is a character or mark that is used to typify something else, and to represent an object or an idea. In symbols we find some degree both of concealment and of revelation.

Throughout many ages of incarnations we have developed an instinctual or subconscious reaction to the forms and shapes around us, until we have come to recognize them as patterns and reflections of the working processes of Cosmic activity. "God geometrizes," we quote; but let us go further to consider how these basic designs express Cosmic Law.

Line formations imply not only shape, but also action, radiation and gravitation, involution and evolution, and many other modes of life action. All design emanates from the line. But before any line can be drawn, the process has to start with a dot (•), the first point of contact between pen and paper. This out-pictures the first "drop" of an idea into the pool of Mind, and becomes the Source or place where the whole creative effort begins.

The force and power of Will to act or create drives this dot to extend itself across the paper, and in the case of a horoscope, the line moves due east (left) to the place where day light begins on the horizon.

One explanation for the design of the horoscope wheel is that ancient Egyptians when worshipping their gods faced south, which they called forward or upward. At their back lay the north, which they called the lower or hinder region. At their left was east, which became the rising sign as it is the point where the sun rises.

Since every circle has but one Center and one radius, the line or radius which emanates from the Center becomes the Ascendant of the chart, or the I AM as manifestation of the Archetype. This line extends to the potential circumference of that individual, or as you might say to the boundary of his atmosphere. The line of the Ascendant becomes the active personality of the Creation, or the starter and doer of this microcosm.

The contact of line with circumference of this invisible circle outlines his sphere of influence as the objectification of the I AM in physical birth. The completed circle shows manifested fulfillment of all the inherent perfection whose potential was contained in the central point of Source. Because we know that we exist at one end of the line, we must also recognize the existence of God at the other end, as the Source of this emanation.

If you learn the simple component parts of the more complex symbols, it becomes possible to dissect them for better understanding, and to come up with more than is in books. Here are given meanings of the most basic forms with which symbolism deals. The dot, straight line, and circle are all there is to start with. And the three fundamental symbols through which the Word of God and the work of Creation manifest are the circle, the triangle, and the square. From these all things evolve.

THE DOT •

The meaning of the dot or central point of a circle is that of Seed, Essence, Nucleus, or Cause. In the horoscope, it represents the God-Spark, or one's "portion of Divinity." It is that point in the egg from which Life begins to manifest. It is the germ, the seed or starting point of a lesser light within the larger, the nucleus of life in all cells. The central point is the Archetype of any idea.

THE CIRCLE ◯

The Circle represents the oversoul; the Creator; God without beginning or end, enclosing His universe. It shows that which is Infinite and boundless as Unmanifested Life or Spirit, Cosmic Mind and Cosmic Force. The perfect circle is a spiritual symbol of the realization of perfection and the fulfillment of potentials, along with release from bondage to form. Only in the circle is the circumference at all times equidistant from the center; for in any figure drawn with straight lines, a degree of crystallization is present, and therefore a static condition, with the movement around the center not constant. The empty circle also implies the feminine principle of the universe, in limitless potential.

THE SEMI-CIRCLE ∪

When upturned, this is called the chalice of the soul, lifting itself in receptivity to God to be filled from on High. It is a symbol of instinct or intuition, as well. The cup shape indicates a passive receptacle, one which reflects that which is above, or receptivity to higher wisdom. When turned on edge as a lunar crescent, it may represent the soul or instinctive mind facing backward or forward.

THE STRAIGHT LINE ——

The drawing of a line from the point indicates the action necessary for manifesting the Archetype. The line is an extension of positive radiant energy from the central point, or the first emanation from Source. As the radius of a circle, it is one spoke of a wheel, or marking point of 1/12 of the zodiac. Two parallel lines indicate polar opposites, or positive and negative.

By itself, the horizontal line represents the rod, and matter or the material plane. It also indicates the spine of animals and unconscious life.

The vertical line indicates spirit in action, as well as the staff, the upright body of man, and the spinal column of man, through which the force of Creation moves.

The wavy or zig-zag line indicates vibratory action, sometimes lightning or electricity, which shakes or breaks up the even tenor of things. Two of these lines used together are the symbol for dissolving or dissolution, the returning of vital components to their original state.

THE CROSS +

The cross combines both horizontal and vertical lines, and unites them. It combines the rod and the staff. It shows the material world as the horizontal line, influenced by Spirit. Divine Love descending through natural life. Sometimes it is called merely the cross of matter, as the meeting point of the four elements of creation. It relates to the number four as does the square, a material number, but the cross implies vital action, and union, as the square does not. When held to matter, spirit must manifest its creative forces in material ways. Planets placed in *T* or cross formation in a horoscope can indicate poles or stresses in life—character builders.

THE SQUARE ☐

Literally the triangle precedes the square, but to continue the discussion of the number four we place it here. The square represents the Cube, as evolution of the solid, comprised of the four elements of Creation. It indicates foundation and base, as the most solid of figures. The four right angles of the square appear as the enclosed reflections of the central angles of the spokes of a wheel, and suggest inflexible boundaries. It implies the taking on of responsibility in that it has already reached perfection with the number 3, and has now carried voluntarily beyond that to establish a foundation for something more to be built upon it. The square relates to measurement and the establishment of Order, and to the four Fixed signs of the zodiac.

The square ☐ aspect in astrology indicates two planets at right angles from each other in the horoscope, and inclined to "butt heads" together, good for impetus or drive, makes stumbling stones into building blocks, but it must be controlled and harmonized.

THE TRIANGLE △

The Triangle is considered a perfect figure, signifying the completion of something. It represents spirit in three modes of expression—that is, will, wisdom, and activity. It represents both positive and negative polarities plus the result of their interaction, or the son, indicating the completed family, As the Holy Family, it is Father, Son, and Holy Spirit. The triangle is symbolic of the Law which is used in prayer. The Grand Trine aspect in astrology, occurs between planets placed 120 degrees or one-third of the circle apart. This aspect is considered one of the most harmonious among planetary relationships and has the effect of a cushion or "earned crown" to the one in whose horoscope it is found. However, by itself it inclines the person to slide by on his luck, and to relax more than is good for evolutionary growth.

The sextile ✳ , or 60-degree aspect, is half that distance and also considered fortunate, an aspect of opportunity.

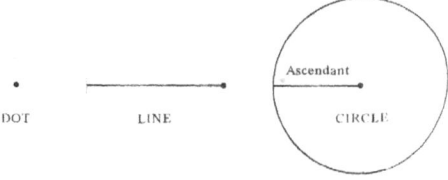

DOT   LINE   Ascendant   CIRCLE

ASTROLOGICAL CORRESPONDENCES OF THE HUMAN BODY

♈ **Aries:** Red. Head, eyes, red corpuscles; (Epilepsy, wounds, accidents).

♉ **Taurus:** Red-orange. Throat, thymus gland; (Goiter, obesity, voice problems).

♊ **Gemini:** Orange. Hands, arms, lungs; (Bronchitis, nervous disorders, tuberculosis).

♋ **Cancer:** Orange-yellow. Stomach, breast; (Digestive ailments, female disorders).

♌ **Leo:** Yellow. Heart, back; (Heart disorders, poor circulation).

♍ **Virgo:** Yellow-green. Small intestine; (Intestinal disorders).

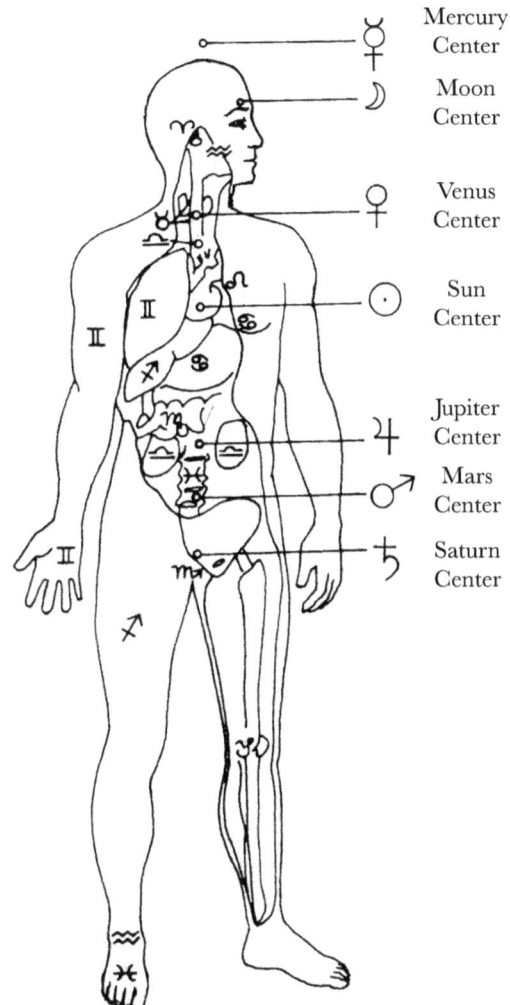

Mercury Center

Moon Center

Venus Center

Sun Center

Jupiter Center

Mars Center

Saturn Center

♎ **Libra:** Green. Kidneys, thymus gland; (Kidney trouble).

♏ **Scorpio:** Green-blue. External generative organs; (Ruptures, venereal disease, toxic complaints).

♐ **Sagittarius:** Blue. Liver, thighs; (Rheumatism, sciatica).

♑ **Capricorn:** Blue-violet. Skin, skeleton, knees; (Arthritis, dislocated bones).

♒ **Aquarius:** Violet. Ankles, ethers in body, pituitary body, magnetic aura; (Broken ankles, nervous diseases).

♓ **Pisces:** Violet-red. Feet, spinal cords, charkas, telepathic functions, superphysical impulses; (Foot troubles, alcoholism or drugs).

PLANETS

PLANETS

The solar system, so far as present knowledge extends, consists of the sun and nine major planets. There are also several thousand asteroids; satellites of planets, or moons; comets, an average of about five per year; meteors or shooting "stars;" and interplanetary dust.

Astrologers find it convenient when dealing with horoscopes to refer to the sun and moon as "planets;" but actually the Sun is a Star, in that it is self-luminous—as are all the countless stars of the sky, which are called "fixed stars" because they appear to our vision as set in one place, due to the immensity of their distances from Earth. Factually, stars are also in motion, and subject to the gravitational control of their own particular systems. Stars, or Suns, are said to be completely gaseous, unlike those planets which consist of solid matter.

This matter may have been originally expelled from the sun, and gradually cooled at a distance from its radiant Source, but the planets are still held in course by this Sun which is the core of their existence, and on Earth the giver of Life itself.

Planets are satellites of the sun, and as such are said to represent "focal points of unconscious energies," or "archetypal impulses associated with basic life-principles." They symbolize basic human functions all regulated and integrated by the sun, expressing through the attitude of the sign they occupy. Man, too, is an energy-system, and through the functioning of these life-principles within him, he is related to the infinite Cosmic energy-systems.

Members of our solar system, including the sun, rotate on their axes from West to East, or in counter-clockwise direction, except Venus, which spins clockwise. All orbit around the sun in an elliptical path, all inclined less than seven degrees from the plane of Earth's path, except Pluto, whose orbit is inclined 17 degrees to that of Earth.

The word "planet" derives from the Greek "*Planetes*" meaning "wanderer." There was an ancient belief that the stars were the bodies of Great and Wise Beings and were considered divine.

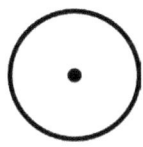

SUN

Metal: Gold
Color: Gold (sometimes orange or yellow)
Rulership: Leo

Michael is usually called the Archangel of the **Sun**, his name translating as "Like unto God."

Many peoples have worshipped the Sun, or a Sun-god, recognizing in its light the life-giving potential. In Egypt, he was called Ra, and his symbol was a winged disk; in Persia, Mithras. The Greek sun god was Helios, whose radiant palace gleamed with gold, ivory and jewels. Few mortals could endure the brilliant light of that place which always shone at high noon when he sat on his splendid throne.

He had four (or nine) winged horses of dazzling white which breathed forth flames, and a golden chariot fashioned by Vulcan, which he would mount early each day as the eastern sky began to purple, and Dawn would open her rosy courts to watch the stars depart, one by one. Then would Helios rise from the eastern seas. The gatekeepers at Olympus, called Seasons, would fling wide the gates for him to rush swifter than wind upward through the mist into higher, clear atmosphere. His flaming steeds needed careful guidance across the heights whence he radiated Light and Life to all upon Earth. These horses symbolize solar energies.

Each night he was received by the western seas in a barque, or golden ship, also fashioned by Vulcan, in which his family awaited, and they sailed all night, reaching the eastern ocean again by morning to launch into orbit. Being the god of light, nothing was secret or hid from him, so he saw all things.

Phoebus Apollo was not really a sun-god, but a god of sunshine, music, and poetry. He was the brother of Phoebe, or Diana, and was first teacher of the healing arts. His unrivalled shrine was the Oracle at Delphi.

⊙ The symbol of the Sun is a circle with a dot in the center—the Creator plus creative Word or seed. Also, the heart of man as the central dynamo of his body. The sun personifies man's life and spirit, given him by the All-Spirit above.

Declaration:

"I will not be a heartbroken, helpless victim of so-called human 'love,' but will learn to control and direct true godly Love; I will radiate from within the Light of Christ, to become a shining lamp for all who are in need."

The Sun in the chart of the individual represents the Source within; the Life-impelling Force which motivates and sustains him; the particular type of expression which he came to experience in this incarnation, and the compelling Force within one which gives drive to the other planets and holds them on their course.

Science Says:

The sun is an "average" Star, but the most important member of *our* Solar System. Truly the only begotten of God in this system, it is the only self-luminous body (except the comets) and the only one which gives light and heat. The planets only reflect and absorb this and depend on the Sun as their source.

The sun easily controls the planets, containing over 99% of all the mass in the solar system. To quote scientists, our sun is said to be a rotating globe of intensely hot gases—55% hydrogen, 44% helium, and 1% of other elements. While our earthly atmosphere consists mainly of oxygen and nitrogen, that of the sun also includes vaporized metals, gaseous iron, lead, zinc, etc. The temperature is said to be 10,000 degrees Fahrenheit at the surface, and millions of degrees at the center. Its diameter is 109 times that of the earth, and it could swallow a million planets our size. Its "mean density" is about one quarter that of Earth.

Whereas the earth receives only one-sixth horse power per square foot of solar radiation, each square foot of the sun's surface radiates 8,000 horse power of energy. The amount received by Earth means the difference between life and death. The records of more than a billion years of continuous sunshine shedding its life-giving warmth on the earth is sealed up in our rocks.

There are differences in solar radiation from season to season due to the angle at which the sun's rays enter Earth's atmosphere. In the Northern Hemisphere they are less in winter and morning or evening, because rays are slanted then; more at noon and midsummer because their angle is more direct. This is the opposite in the Southern Hemisphere. The intensity of radiation also increases with the growth of sun spots—that is, cyclonic masses of electricity-charged particles which are bombarded into space from the sun at the speed of light, and at such times the amount of ultra-violet rays entering the earth's atmosphere may be doubled. This affects the intensity of electrical storms, and Earth's magnetism, as well as weather, plant growth, and economic conditions. Sun spots occur in an eleven-year cycle, but alternative positive and negative polarities make them noticeably effective mainly on the positive cycle, or every 22 years.

One theory of sun spots is that planets by their mutual action set off a sort of composite tidal wave on the sun's surface, setting the solar atmosphere into "oscillation." War or depression has often occurred at periods of low sun-spot activity, at 22-year intervals. It is known that death occurs more often in early morning hours after man has been cut off from solar radiation for hours.

VULCAN

Vulcan is not a planet used by astrologers, due to lack of data concerning its course. It was estimated to be not more than eight and one-half degrees from the sun (from our viewing range) but anything that close is next to invisible to earthly vision. However, there had been observations of what was accepted as an intra-Mercurial planet (within the orb of Mercury, the closest visible planet to the sun), and in 1857 a group of astronomers discussing this planet named it Vulcan. This theory was disproved in 1915 when the anomalies to Mercury's orbit were attributed to Einstein's theory of relativity. But that may not be the end of the story. Vulcan is an integral part of humanity's evolution. So, we will wait and see what future scientific developments may arise before making a final determination.

The name was derived from a myth which correlates with the nature of the planet. Any planet so close to the sun must be very hot, so Vulcan as the mythological worker of hot iron, a blacksmith-god, was chosen. Vulcan, also called Hephaestus, was the Greek god of Fire, and son of Hera, who is said to have borne him in answer to Jupiter's having brought forth Athena alone.

He was the only one among the gods who was ugly and lame. In turn, each of his parents cast him from heaven, but he remained to become honored as the workman of the immortals, their armorer and metal-smith, god of forge, of Fire, and of metallurgy. He made for them dwellings, furnishings, and weapons. In his workshop he forged golden maidens who could move and help him with his work.

He was kindly, peace-loving, and popular in earth and heaven. He and Athena were both very important in city life, both being patrons of handicrafts and the arts; he was protector of smiths, and she of weavers.

Vulcan's wife was the beautiful Venus who had other lovers, one of whom was Mars. Vulcan made sport of him on Mt. Olympus and it appears that this invisible planet near the sun has a detrimental effect on the planet Mars, even from the standpoint of science.

Certain weather prophets who use Vulcan in their observations concur that it controls the air currents on the surface of Earth. This agrees with the tradition that Vulcan was father of Ethiops, which mean "ether" or "thin air."

Some astrologers have claimed that a planet found in one's horoscope within eight and one-half degrees of the sun was in "combustion" and its virtue or characteristics burned up or destroyed in that position. This only holds true part of the time; therefore it would appear that this action would occur only if there was a conjunction to Vulcan at the same time, as it moves in its path around the sun.

The Egyptian representation of this character was a spotted leopard carrying on its back a winged human head, said to refer to Vulcan "riding the Sun." Later, in Greece this was changed to Bacchus riding on a panther.

MERCURY
Metal: Quicksilver
Color: Yellow
Rulership: Gemini and Virgo

Mercury is the closest planet to the sun that is visible to our eyes, yet so close to the sun as to be seldom seen. It is believed to have little atmosphere, which accounts for its reflecting only 7% of the sunlight received. Its 7-degree inclination to the ecliptic (off-course) is surpassed only by Pluto. Despite its symbolic swiftness, Mercury turns slowly on its axis—one day on this planet being equal to 88 earth days, or as some believe, 58 days. Its year is also 88 days in length.

The symbol is composed of a circle, placed over a cross, with a lunar crescent or half-circle above. It is both a solar and lunar symbol, with power to dominate the elements.

Between the Cross of Matter and the subconscious receptively upturned, lies a circle showing the potential of Mind, more or less brought forth and stimulated by the other two. Its symbol in botany indicates a hermaphroditic, or perfect plant or flower, bisexual.

☿ The Crescent signifies the cup of the Soul upturned to receive from above; the qualities of the Moon, which are receptive, reflective and passive. The whole suggests balanced forces, with receptivity to wisdom from above. It is a semi-circle, representing the receptive subconscious.

╬ The Cross stands for physical matter, or expressions in the physical and impact from the physical world. It also signifies the four elements meeting at (or proceeding from) a common center. The active power of generation and passive power of production are conjoined in the cross, as are the equator and equinoctial.

◯ The Circle signifies cosmic force, or cosmic Mind—the Cosmos: Unmanifest God; or the fire of Life.

☿ Another of its symbols is the caduceus composed of twin serpents twined about a winged staff, used as a healing symbol by physicians today. This suggests Mercury's rulership of not only Gemini the Twins, but also of Virgo, sign of health and of healing. The wings represent the crossbar of Mercury, the serpents' heads forming a crescent at the top. The caduceus was carried by the important gods and goddesses of Mind, such as Hermes, Mercury, Cybele, Minerva, and Anubis or Thoth.

Mercury endows one with love of things intellectual, with quickness of mind, and interest in correct phraseology. It is the planet of the Intellect or reasoning mind, the Architect, Alchemist, and the Magician, whose work is to initiate all action in mind.

The power to think distinguishes man from the animal. None of the air signs among the constellations is symbolized by an animal. Man's mind comes into contact with all things, however distant. The Egyptian version of Mercury, called Thoth or Anubis, was the conductor of souls on their journey between earth and the astral realms—performing an important work as guide of the "dead."

In Greek mythology, he was a son of Zeus (Jupiter), and of Maia, a daughter of Atlas. As messenger of the gods on Olympus, he *flew swift as thought* to do their bidding, with wings on sandals, helmet, and wand helping to speed his way. He was both swift and graceful, cunning, shrewd, and quick-witted. He acted as god of commerce, marketing, trade, and as protector of those employed therewith. Before he was one day old, he had stolen the herds of Apollo, but his father made him return them, and appeased Apollo by giving him a lyre. Mercury is called a hermaphroditic sign. Raphael is usually considered its archangel, and his name means "God the Healer."

One with this planet strong must declare, "I will not be turned aside by cold logic or literal factualism from perceiving the Truth, which can only be known from within, nor from the inspiration that must be spiritually, not mentally, received. I will use my mind as the marvelous tool it is for construction and communication.

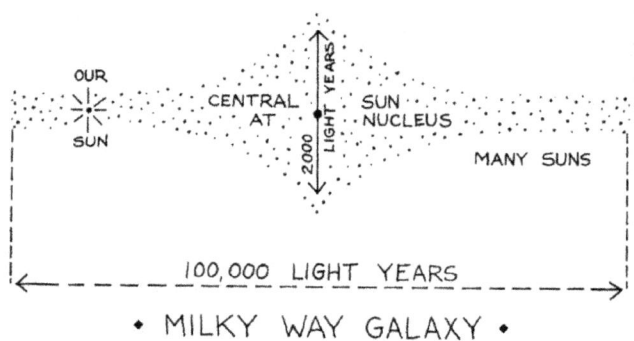

VENUS
Metals: Copper, Brass and Bronze
Color: Green
Rulership: Taurus and Libra

"Love one another, even as I have loved you..."

Moving inside of Earth's path around the sun is our nearest neighbor, **Venus**, sometimes called the twin of Earth. Her brilliance in our eyes is second only to that of the sun and moon, and about ten times that of the brightest Star, Sirius. This brightness is due to increased reflection of sunlight from its denser atmosphere and the clouds which surround it. This cloud-veil of mystery symbolizes the eternal feminine aspect, and the veil of Isis, and should aid the planet in keeping out excess heat by day, and blanket in the solar heat at night.

Venus is never more than 47 degrees east or west of the sun, and is "evening star" or "morning star," depending on whether it is west of and rising before the sun, or east of and setting after the sun.

Azrael (Anael, or Hanael) is said to be the archangel of the planet Venus; the name means "Grace of God."

Venus was the mythical goddess of Love and Beauty, also called Aphrodite, and her sweet laughter beguiled all who saw her, whether gods or men. She even stole the wits of the wise, and laughed at those who succumbed to her wiles. She is sometimes called the daughter of Zeus and Dione, but is usually said to have been born when a drop of her father's blood fell from heaven into the sea, and she sprang full-blown from sea foam. The Greek word *Aphros* means "foam," and her name is explained as meaning "foam-risen" or "foam-born." This occurred near the Isle of Cyprus, and these islands became sacred to her in after times, the cypress being called her tree. She was sometimes known as Cytherea, and was the wife of Vulcan.

Negatively, she was counted treacherous and malicious, with power to destroy men with her wiles.

But positively, at her coming winds and storm clouds would flee, the flowers bloom, the seas and meadows laugh, and Beauty and Joy would present themselves in the radiant loveliness of her presence.

Myrtle and dove, sparrow and swan, were some of her symbols, as were the rose and apple.

Her symbol shows a cross surmounted by a circle. This indicates the spiritual aspect placed above the material, so spiritual force is put in control of matter, and able to use the elements, or balance of rod and staff. Masculine and feminine qualities combine, surmounted by Creator as Head. Sometimes the circle is considered a solar symbol. Cross and circle together show the energization of Earth from above, to cause vegetation and animal life. It depicts the cosmic force of the feminine in its generative aspect, the fruitful Mother of Nature. In botany this symbol depicts the female organism or cell, the pistillate plant or flower.

Attributes of Venus are artistic refinement, harmony, grace, charm, beauty and love; material Plenty. Those with Venus negatively emphasized may be self-indulgent, wasteful, and slovenly; displaying misapplied love, or self-gratification without regard for others.

The Seven Wonders of the ancient world are said to have been erected by an Order of Initiate Builders as monuments to the seven known planets, counting the sun as one. This indicates a widespread knowledge of the Heavenly Mysteries in times of old.

An altar to the sun was the Colossus of Rhodes; the temple of Diana at Ephesus was dedicated to the moon; the Great Pyramid is considered as dedicated to Mercury; the hanging gardens of Semiramis to Venus; the mausoleum of Halicarnassus was in honor of Mars; the Olympian Zeus was to Jupiter; and the Pharos of Alexandria was to Saturn.

Venus should declare:

"I will not spend efforts toward adornment or allure to satisfy my ego, or to draw others under my spell of enchantment, but will learn to listen and to give, to love wisely and selflessly—God first, and the good of all."

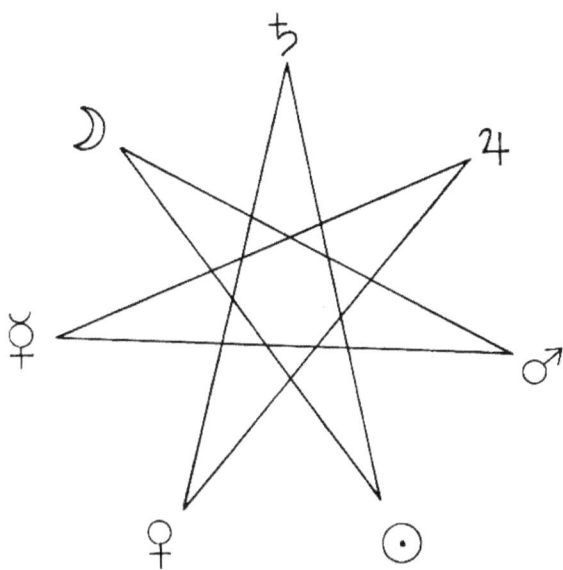

Star of Venus (Ishtar)

Earth and Moon
Moon Metal: Silver
Moon Color: Blue or White
Moon Rules: Cancer

The **Moon** is a satellite of the **Earth,** and thus they must be treated as one unit, where the solar system is concerned. The earth, like all planets, rotates on its axis from west to east, so that other heavenly bodies appear to be moving from east to west. Its movements once annually around the sun is from west to east, its orbit inclined 23 and one-half degrees to the plane of its equator, all of which cause seasons and climactic differences. These in turn have quite definite biological and physiological effects on humans.

The earth is called an oblate spheroid because it is slightly flattened at its poles and bulges at the equator. Its size and type of materials cause *gravity*, or *holding power*, and permit sufficient atmosphere with the oxygen we breathe to support life. Our temperate climate is due to being located neither too far from nor too near the sun. A layer of ozone in the upper atmosphere screens out most of the sun's destructive ultraviolet light. This atmospheric layer also prevents a drastic temperature change of several hundred degrees between day and night, which would be unbearable; and it helps retain the moisture which permits growth and prevents the earth from becoming a desert. Radio communication is made possible by the electrified portion of our atmosphere called ionosphere. This is in turn affected by sun spots and coronal mass ejections, which sometimes make circuit changes necessary that communications may not be disrupted.

⊕ The symbol for Earth is a cross contained within a circle, or spirit enclosing and containing matter within itself; the elements bound together by spirit. Other symbols used astronomically are ⊖ and ♁ (circle with inverted T above). Earth does not appear as a planet in our horoscope, because the wheel is set up from the view point of our location on the earth's surface, and standing on it, we do not observe it in the heavens. The rising sign is shown as the Ascendant on the eastern horizon, and the spot directly overhead is the tenth cusp or Midheaven.

Mythologically, Mother Earth was called Gaia, wife of Ouranos ("heaven"). Rhea, wife of Saturn, was later goddess of Earth. Another name for her was Ops. The wife of Jupiter, or Zeus, was goddess of all matters pertaining to women and motherhood. Her name was Juno, or Hera.

The earth is most important to us, because it is our home and base of operations, and the only planet we know as yet for living purposes. From it, all our measurements are made of time and space, and these are put in terms relative to what we know here.

Moon

The moon is intimately associated with the earth; it may actually be the mother or twin planet of ancient times, if the rocks being studied are any criterion. The two were possibly one body at some time in the past.

Due to lack of moisture and atmosphere, the moon is unprotected from bombardment by the sun's rays, and so far as man's eyes and limited human concepts have been able to detect, it is not supposed to support life.

Nodes

The moon is the earth's satellite, revolving around it in about 27 and one-third days, in an elliptical path whose orbit is inclined five degrees and eight minutes from the plane of the earth's orbit. *The points of intersection* where the moon's path crosses the earth's orbit around the sun *are called Nodes.* The sun must be near a node to produce either a *solar or lunar eclipse.*

The quality of the ascending or North Node ☊, also known as the Dragon's head, is considered benefic similar to a conjunction with Jupiter, while the quality of the descending or South Node ☋ , also known as the Dragon's tail, is considered of the nature of a conjunction with Saturn, and somewhat restrictive in effect. The nodes are not greatly considered in the natal chart unless in close conjunction with a planet or important point, since they are not factually existent. However, they are considered "sensitive points" in a horoscope.

Moon and Earth are revolving simultaneously, so the actual time it takes the moon to complete its reunion with the sun (from the viewpoint of the earth) is *29½ days, called the synodic month* which extends from one New Moon to the next.

In fact, the moon and Earth revolve around each other, and that which follows the path of the earth's orbit is the *center of mass of the two.* The daily variations of Earth's magnetism are caused by changes in solar and lunar influences. In late fall and early winter, the magnetism is amplified to about 70% after New and Full Moons, from what it is four days after the first and third quarters. This seems directly due to effects of tidal motions of the atmosphere. It is also the moon's gravitational pull on the earth which causes the ocean's tides.

While moonlight is 300,000 times less intense than sunlight, radio waves change a great deal between the New Moon and the full, the number of microvolts nearly doubling during that time, caused by abnormal reflections from the E layer of the ionosphere around the time of Full Moon, when it is most bright, and New Moon, when its light becomes almost non-existent from Earth's standpoint.

Stonehenge in England was apparently a kind of observatory which enabled priests to announce the coming seasons and eclipses of sun and moon, and to celebrate the religious rituals which commemorated them. It is thought to have been built about 1800 B.C.

Its upright stones are 12 feet high, with 56 pits around them. The crude ruins can still be used to record positions of sun and moon quite precisely, the results not more than one degree of a circle off, plus or minus.

Mythically, the moon was represented by the goddess Diana, also called Artemis, chief Huntress of the gods and the protectress of youth. Cypress, deer and other wild animals were sacred to her. She used silver arrows, silver being the metal of the moon. She was also called Phoebe, and was the twin sister of Phoebus Apollo, god of Truth and Light. The moon is given three forms—in the underworld, she is Hecate, associated with darkness both of night and moon, and of deed when light is hidden and evil magic stalks ghostly places.

On the earth plane, she is known as Artemis, "Great is Artemis of the Ephesians," Paul was told. The Hebrew Jericho was also a city of the moon.

In Heaven, she is called Selene, who was sister of Helios the sun god.

Several of the gods of ancient Egypt were thought to represent the moon, which was quite important in their lore. Its waxing phase was called "the opening of Horus' eye," and when it was full the eye of the hawk-god was said to be completely open. The cycle of the moon, around 28 days, compared to a staircase of 14 steps; first one ascended the staircase to the fullness of the Open Eye, then one went down the fourteen steps until the eye closed at New Moon.

First quarter moon is $\mathcal{D}$; last quarter moon $\mathbb{C}$; astrologers use the former. The moon's symbol is a crescent resembling a new moon. Its cup shape depicts that which is open to receive, a passive receptacle. Its silvery nature shows the quality of reflection and conductivity. Whereas the sun shines steadily of itself, the moon only lights up at anything which shines upon it, and acts as a mirror both for positive and negative situations. While in its physical state it is considered dry and lifeless; yet it symbolizes water and the nurturing of life. It represents the soul and the subconscious mind upon which memories are inscribed and the storehouse where all experiences are kept. From out of this store of memory and experience spring man's instincts and intuitions, his emotions, imagination, and the reactions (like reflections) to all that occurs. It has a passive quality.

The moon in a chart represents the soul, and the intuitive qualities, the family history, impulses and instincts, the memory of olden times. It shows the personality as reflection of the Individuality, and the subjective mind turned inward toward Spirit, then projected outward toward the World. It represents the feminine ideal, or the mother image or women as a whole. It may also signify the "people" or the public in general.

Uriel is considered archangel of the earth, while Gabriel is archangel of the moon. The meaning of Uriel is said to be "Light of God," the Hebrew "Ur" means "shining." Gabriel means "Strength of God," with the suggestion of procreation.

Declaration:

"I will not react or be ruffled by every whimsical breeze, neither will I reflect the negation of others, or match it with like. I will hold sacred all mysteries revealed to me, and will use them for good."

The moon, as ruler of the sign Cancer, is called the mother of all things, patroness of the life forces of nature, and the origin of all life.

The symbolism of the moon placed under the feet of the Virgin is in reference to the moon's exaltation in Taurus, a sign of love; its form shows the horns of the Bull.

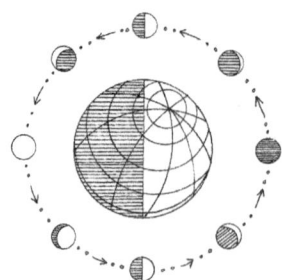

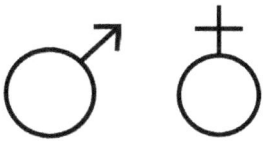

MARS
Metal: Iron or Steel
Color: Red
Rulership: Aries

The symbol of **Mars** is the reverse of Venus, as its color is also opposite. Mars places its cross (+) above the circle, showing matter as emerging upward, expelled outward, from the solar (o) or spiritual potential which feeds it from below. Thus, it denotes the creation of matter emerging from the sun, and the solar aspects dominated by the physical. It shows the masculine potential propelled into action, first toward material conditions, and the creative energy which spurs man into action. It is directly concerned with the sensations and the muscles. The first impulse generated in the physical makes for aggressiveness.

In botany, this symbol refers to the male organism or cell, the staminate plant or flower. Its cross is usually depicted as an arrowhead, which brings out the intensity and speed of action. Mars energy is not mental, but rather athletic or fiery in nature. Martian.

The Roman Mars was the Greek Ares, lover of Venus. His animal was the dog, his bird the vulture. He was son of Jupiter and Juno (Zeus and Hera) and his sister was Discord; her son, Strife. These brought groaning and blood to the earth, for Mars was the god of War.

To the Romans he was glorious, and their very weapons were sacred emblems to the warriors who believed that death on the battlefield was glorious. They considered him magnificent, an invincible warrior in shining armor. Samael or Kamael is his archangel, and means "Severity of God."

Mars is called the power which constitutes the framework of creation, therefore creativity and new outpourings of energy, sometimes in destruction, but also in construction. It depicts the sex energies in their natural form as the root of other powers, and as the ceaseless stream of energy which brings about new forms in nature. It has to do with continual activity, and is the exciting influence which gives the initial impulse to various trains of action. When lifted up in the spiritual individual, it leads to regeneration. Man, or masculinity, is generated by the cosmic Mars forces.

Where Mars is found in the horoscope will be the urge to action or aggression. In a woman's chart it may depict the type of sweetheart to which she would be drawn. Afflicted it may incline to accidents, or burns, or impetuous aggressive action, or temper.

The planet itself appears red in the heavens, and is quite bright. Its atmosphere is believed to be more rare than Earth's, its day slightly longer than ours, its seasons similar, but almost twice as long. It has two moons. Something which appears like thin ice at the poles "melts" with the seasons; and darker areas then spread, which look from here like vegetation.

Declaration:

"I will not 'fall' in love, hate nor anger, and will not allow selfish passion to overcome judgment; I will direct energy upward in constructive action and get things done for the glory of God and the betterment of mankind."

PYTHAGORAS

Pythagoras of the Sixth Century B.C., and certain other Greek philosophers, dared teach that the Sun was the center of the universe, and that the earth revolved around it, but their views carried little weight on that point.

PTOLEMY

There were three pre-Christian kings of Egypt by that name, but the originator of the Ptolemaic System was a Greek mathematician of the second century, who lived in Alexandria. Ptolemy declared that the earth was the central body around which the sun, planets, and other celestial bodies revolved. Though he was not the first to accept this, he did write an excellent book in which he reported his own findings and calculations along with the findings of all those who had come before him, so that his book now provides scholars with one of the few records of ancient calculations. His system was taught, without dispute, from 140 AD. until 1543.

COPERNICUS

1543 A.D. was a great date in science, for in that year, the Polish-German astronomer Copernicus published his treatise now known as the Copernicus Theory:

"...The earth is not the center of the universe."

"All the planets revolve around the sun; the sun, therefore is the center of the solar system."

"... What appears to us to be motion of the sun (stems not) from its motions, but from the motions of the earth."

"The earth revolves around the sun like any other planet."

These beliefs ran counter to those accepted in his day, but he diagrammed the paths of the planets and the moon with amazing accuracy, even calculating the length of the year to within 28 minutes—all this before the invention of a telescope.

GALILEO

It was 21 years later, in 1564 AD., that Galileo was born, and he became a believer in the Copernican Theory. Hearing of a Dutch lens-maker who had invented a lens which could identify distant objects, he investigated and through this he invented the first telescope, with which he made great astronomical discoveries. He died the year another great scientist, Isaac Newton, was born.

♃

JUPITER
Metal: Tin
Color: Blue or Purple
Rulership: Sagittarius

Jupiter is the largest of all the planets in the solar system, its mass exceeding that of all the others combined; yet it rotates fastest, turning on its axis in only 10 hours, which causes a large bulge at its equator. Its 12 moons, two of them larger than Mercury, and two the size of our moon, were discovered by Galileo in 1610 with the first telescope. Its deep atmosphere is believed to be made up of much ammonia and methane; visibly there are bands or "belts" of clouds in brown, yellow, and orange, parallel to the equator. It is probably very cold, due to its distance from the sun. One scientist believes that equinoctial disturbances on Jupiter affect the sun, and through this the solar system, resulting in increase of electric intensity.

The King of Planets remains in each constellation about one year, requiring 12 years to circle around the sun. Zeus or Jupiter was Lord of the Sky, Rain god and Cloud gatherer. He wielded the mighty thunderbolt, his power greater than all others, so he was also king of the gods who ruled everything in heaven including weather, the thunder and lightning. In the sunny lands where he ruled, rain was the precious water of Life. His priests wore white caps, his chariot was drawn by four white horses, and white animals were sacrificed at his feasts or rituals. "The seven thunders uttered things which the seers were forbidden to write."

His wife was Hera or Juno, faithful, but jealous of his many amorous adventures. Zeus was a composite god, the tales of many gods of many lands being brought together as people mingled and, in a sense, they made him out in their own image, zestful, adventurous, and little mindful of morals. He was also called "giver of good gifts," being generous and hospitable.

His father was Saturn, who swallowed his children as soon as they were born, because it had been predicted that one of them would succeed him. But when the sixth was born, his wife Rhea hid the child and gave her husband a swaddled stone to swallow. When the child was grown, he came and overthrew his father and took the throne, first making him disgorge the other children. Even in the time of Paul, bulls were being sacrificed to Jupiter. His bird was the eagle, his tree the oak, and his oracle was Dodona in the land of oak trees. Priests interpreted his wishes by the rustling of oak leaves. The Bible mentions sacred oak groves of the pagans.

The symbol ♃ for Jupiter consists of a crescent or half-circle facing left, and resting at the left edge of the horizontal bar of a cross. Though conjoined, the mental aspect of the semicircle is foremost, the cross second. He accumulates at the center and expands outward into greater experience, facing out from the cross of matter. It indicates balanced forces, receptively expressed, yet outgoing. The lunar aspect of Jupiter (semicircle) is able to dominate the elements (cross). The elevated aspect of the moon signifies the instinctive consciousness now perfected through lessons learned. It has become soul of the superconscious aspect, rather than of the subconscious.

The archangel of Jupiter is said to be Zadkiel, or Tzadkiel, meaning "righteousness of God."

The characteristics of this planet in the horoscope are the outgoing, outspreading idea of benevolent expansion. It is the traveler ("first class"), the philosopher, the religionist, the outdoorsman, the sportsman, or the philanthropist. It shows the big spender, or if afflicted, the over-spender. It indicates comfortable living, or wastefulness, good position, the well-to-do, or the ne'er-do-well, King or hobo, the horseplayer flashily dressed, or the middle-class businessman with a slight paunch who belongs to the best club in town, man-of-affairs, statesman, lawgiver or politician, exponent of theories.

Declaration:

"I will not overindulge in 'good living' but will seek to live the Good life, high-minded, compassionate in well-doing, and moderate in all things."

A noted French doctor claimed that X-rays of great intensity emanate from all the stars. This activity undoubtedly affects the human organism, because the penetrating X-rays affect all atoms, and particularly bodily tissues. These celestial X-rays exercise some influence on all life.

SATURN
Metal: Lead
Color: Indigo (or dark colors)
Rulership: Capricorn

Saturn is the planet next largest to Jupiter, but further away, and less dense. It is supposedly the only planet lighter than water—which is paradoxical, because it is esoterically a planet of earth nature, associated with lead, with contraction and crystallization. It probably has a deep-cold atmosphere of methane and ammonia, and this agrees astrologically with its rulership of ice and snow.

It makes a splendid picture seen through a telescope, due to its three distinct large rings made up of many small particles similar to meteorites, fragments circling in orbit which could be ice particles or a broken moon. These are at the level of Saturn's equator, each 10 miles thick and 10,000 miles wide. A day on the planet is 10 hours and 48 minutes of our time. The planet remains in each constellation about two and one-half years, taking 29 years to circle the sun. It has nine small satellites outside the rings.

Saturn was the outermost planet known to the ancients, and marked the boundary of the solar system to the naked eye. Partly for this reason it became identified with all boundaries and restrictions, of the skin, for example, and of shells or walls which shut out or close in. It represents the principles of contraction and solidification; of form, structure, materialization, or matter in specialized form. It creates the things Jupiter tells others about. As ruler of the skeleton, it produces the form around which matter develops.

Saturn is the recluse and the disciplinarian, the teacher and traditionalist. It refers to the elderly or more responsible type of person, and to the father symbol; it refers to government as a law— and structure—maker.

The symbol of Saturn ♄ shows a material cross standing above and before the semicircle of mind and soul. It is like the Jupiter symbol, except in reverse, because here the cross of matter is placed higher than the lunar aspect, taking precedence and being at the same time turned inward.

Saturn is introspective, and the attention of the receptive mind is turned inward toward the cross. It shows the lunar nature dominated by the earthly elements, but working together to stabilize and materialize. The prominence of the cross shows a need for the spiritual to be brought more into the individual's nature. It has an aspect of taking and holding, drawing in from circumference to center. In this sense it relates to hearing.

The sickle-bearing Saturn (or Cronus) of mythology was originally the god of seedtime and harvest, a protector of those who planted a sowed seed, while his wife Ops (Rhea) was a harvest helper. Together they were the parents or grandparents of the chief gods and goddesses on Mt. Olympus. His son Jupiter later took the throne.

Declaration:

"I will avoid greed or stinginess, sensuality or ideas of enslavement, and will become positive in disposition, cheerful and outgiving in practice, free and freeing."

ASTROLOGY AND SOUND

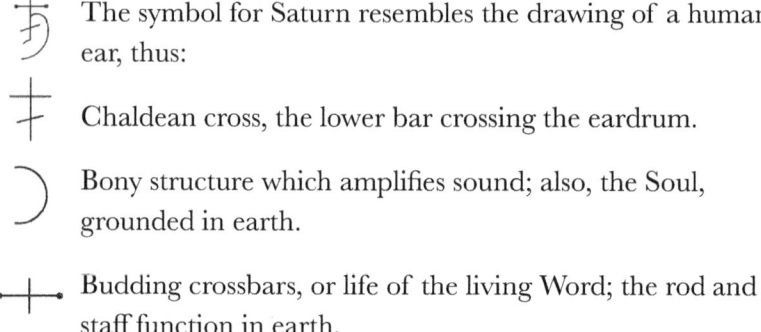

The symbol for Saturn resembles the drawing of a human ear, thus:

Chaldean cross, the lower bar crossing the eardrum.

Bony structure which amplifies sound; also, the Soul, grounded in earth.

Budding crossbars, or life of the living Word; the rod and staff function in earth.

Sound: "Pythagoras conceived the universe to be an immense monochord, its single string being connected at its upper end to absolute Spirit, and its lower end to absolute matter—somewhat as a cord stretched between heaven and earth."

URANUS
Element: Uranium
Electrical Colors
Rulership: Aquarius

Uranus was the first planet ever discovered with a telescope. In 1871, Sir William Herschel, a musician with astronomy as a hobby, made his own telescope and discovered the hitherto unknown planet, twice as far from the sun as Saturn. (This might be considered the first harbinger of the Aquarian Age.) He also gave us the first viewpoint concerning our galaxy the Milky Way, and the Great Nebula in Andromeda.

The plane of its equator is almost at right angles to the plane of its orbit around the sun, causing its five satellites to move almost at right angles to the direction of the planet's motion. It has a thick, cloudy atmosphere. It spends seven years in each sign, 84 years going around the sun; and its day is about ten and three-quarters of our hours long.

The breakthrough past Saturn's supposed "ring-pass-not" into an area beyond the scope of vision explains part of the astrological attributes of Uranus. It represents the breaking-away from old accepted norms of behavior or from rigid control. It brings unexpected insight into the future, and sudden sweeping-away of the past, coming like a flash of lightning to reveal the Truth, at best, or to revolt unreasonably at times. It shakes life out of ruts and brings about whole new patterns and concepts; it is original, inventive and scientific, not emotional. With it comes insight into the laws of nature, and revelation which comes in flashes. Uranus is able to gather up and synthesize the many aspects of intelligence. It relates more to the occult than does Neptune.

The name Uranus, Ouranos, means "heaven"; mythically he was the father of all creatures with his wife Gaea, Mother Earth after Creation. The firstborn creatures were strange and monstrous and Uranus was imprisoning all his children because he did not like them, until one son, Saturn, was bold enough to overcome him and then became king of heaven. The rule of Uranus, through Aquarius, of this age would appear to indicate a replay of the old drama of Creation on a new level—the Creation of a New Heaven and a New Earth.

The symbol for Uranus is threefold: the first is a symbol like Mars, with a dot in the circle, used by astronomers and some European astrologers ♂. The second, ♅ , has two upright pillars joined together by the cross of matter with a small circle or sun suspended from its middle, somewhat like the pendulum of a clock. Man's two bodies are joined by the rod and staff. The third form ♆ uses two moons, one of the human nature and one of the divine, separate, with backs together, joined by the cross. This looks much like a Pisces symbol with pendulum added. All these forms represent the energy of spirit in its play upon matter, or on the other hand, the investigation of matter which results in forms of dynamic energy.

While spirit still manifests through matter, it must be controlled by mind. The two moons represent mind on both sides, the higher and lower working together. More forces working together result in new manifestations not possible to either working singly.

Declaration:

"Let me change, not for the sake of changing, but to replace unsatisfactory or outworn modes and ideas with new and better ones."

 Uranus, the planet ruling electricity.

+) The spiritual body is positive.

(− The physical body is negative.

It is between the spiritual and the physical that the full realization comes.

——— The rod.

| The staff.

The aim of the Aquarian Age is the joining of past and future, and the rising of the principle of fire, which only comes when self-determination ceases, and one says, "Father, here I am without one plea."

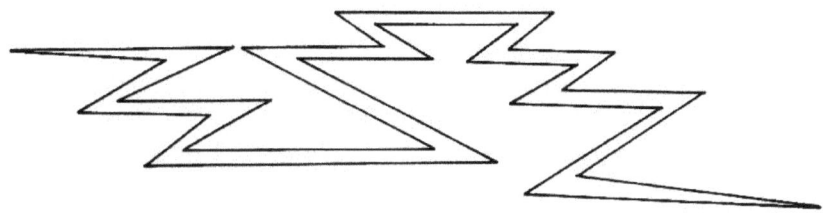

NEPTUNE
Rulership: Pisces

Neptune is similar in size to Uranus, but stays twice as long, or 14 years, in one sign, and is about 10 million miles farther from the sun. Both Uranus and Neptune are ice giants. Neptune is dark, cold, and has storm system and clouds that revolve around the planet. It was discovered in 1843 by mathematical calculation due to a pull on the orbit of Uranus from without, and was named for the god of the sea.

The sea-god Neptune or Poseidon was considered next to his brother Jupiter in importance. The lands around the Mediterranean were dependent on fishing for much of their economy, and the waves and the calm waters were under his command. With his three-pronged spear he could shatter whatever he pleased. He had a magnificent palace beneath the sea, but chose to spend more time on Mt. Olympus. He is said to have made man a gift of the first horse.

His symbol, the trident ♆, conferred on him dominion over the sea and its inhabitants. It represents the three-fold spirit in man reaching upward, and one whose vision is turned upward rather than into earth. It depicts the chalice of the moon pierced through by the staff of the sun. This aids the spirit in its swift penetration to man's conscious mind that he may prophesy, if found worthy. It encourages man to create from the soul, and inspires him to respond to its highly spiritual vibration. For it is considered the most spiritual and mystic of planets, acting beyond the scope of reason or understanding, yet seeming to recognize by wholes rather than by parts. Its symbol also resembles the cup of a flower, its receptacle hiding a secret inner chamber, near the stem.

It carries a misty and nebulous influence, indicating something deep or even secret, covered or misrepresented, and mysterious because too indefinite to be known. It can have the effect of fog in concealing the nature of a thing, yet it also has to do with spiritual Truth, and must be responded to on the spiritual level to keep from having a negative effect, because it is not of an earthly nature. Its lower aspect suggests drugs, anesthetics, alcohol, deception, or self-delusion, but its prominence indicates spiritual potential in the person ready to respond. The sea is also known as the dissolver of form.

Declaration:

"I will not fool myself with charming smoke screens, but seek the spiritual Truth which lies at the core of all happenings."

♇

PLUTO
Rulership: Scorpio

Pluto was discovered February 18, 1930, also through mathematical calculations. Since its revolution around the sun takes 248 years, very little was known of it. Lots more is now known about it with the New Horizon flyby in 2015. This planet is so far distant as to be almost outside the solar system.

Its orbit is more elongated than other planets, and though supposedly about nine million miles beyond the orbit of Neptune, yet it will have moved inside Neptune's path during the years of 1979 to 2000, coming closer to Earth than Neptune during those years. Its stay in the twelve signs varies considerably, unlike other planets. It remains in one sign anywhere from its 12 years in Scorpio, the shortest, to 31 years in Taurus, the longest. It is thought by some to have been a satellite of Neptune which broke away.

The easiest symbol to use for Pluto is the simple contraction of the letters **P** and **L**, ♇ . This is both the initials of its discoverer, Percival Lowell, and the first two letters of the name Pluto. Actually, Lowell made calculations which led to the discovery of the planet after his death. Another symbol is like an elongated Mars symbol, with two small bars across the shaft of the arrow ♂ . This shows its link with Mars as co-ruler of Scorpio, which Pluto replaced as ruler on its discovery. Another commonly used symbol is drawn like a wide-mouthed chalice ♇ , with two cross-bars across its stem, and a tiny circle floating in the cup, its composition being of the sun, the moon, and the cross of matter—or spirit, soul, and body.

The Pluto of mythology was called "Giver of Wealth," and god of the underworld, the lower realms, where he was seated in gloomy majesty on a throne of ebony. In importance, he was third among the gods on Mt. Olympus, after Jupiter and Neptune. Another of his names was Hades. He seldom left the dark realms he ruled, and because of his nature was not often invited, for while not evil, he was inexorable and unpityingly just. He was worshipped but rarely, for he heeded neither sacrifice nor prayer.

He was king of the dead, but not Death itself. His crowded palace stood amid a cold wasteland beyond three rivers which separated his realm from that above. These were the river of fire, the river of unbreakable oath (the river Styx by which gods swear), and the river of forgetfulness, Lethe. The palace was guarded by a three-headed and dragon-tailed dog, Cerberus, who allowed all to enter but none to leave.

Pluto was called the god of every evil and secret deed. Yet he was more than that—the god, for example, of judgment which sends each to its appropriate reward, to torment, or to the delightful Elysian Fields. A boatman ferries souls across a river of lamentation, and ghosts flit about this shadowy place. As god of wealth, Pluto ruled over all things hidden in the depths of earth, precious metals and vaults. He had a cap which made its wearer invisible.

Pluto marks those epochal periods of life when we become suddenly aware of changes which have been in the making, unnoticed for some time. It refers especially to changes in the larger scene which affect numbers or groups of people in society. It deals with elimination, renewal, and transformation. Like the god, it suggests underlying, subterranean activities which eventually force out into the open something which has been agitating from within, so that it may be eliminated or transformed. And it rules the collective subconscious, the deep rumblings of society.

Declaration:

"I'll not be swayed by mob hysteria, regardless of sympathies, but will help wherever the most uplifting results may be accomplished."

❧

SIDEREAL Defined

The word Sidereal is from the Latin "*sidus*," or "*sideris*," meaning "star" and refers to measurements by means of stars.

> **Sidereal Day:** The period of one complete rotation of the earth, with reference to the vernal equinox.

> **Sidereal Hour:** The 24th part of a sidereal day.

> **Sidereal Time:** Time based on rotation of the earth with reference to the vernal equinox.

> **Sidereal Year:** Period of 365 days, six hours, nine minutes, and nine seconds in which time the sun apparently returns to the same position among the fixed stars it held the previous year.

> This is about 21 minutes longer than the Astronomical, or Solar, year we use which is based on one revolution of the earth around the sun in the interval between one vernal equinox and the next—measuring 365 days, five hours, 48 minutes and 46 seconds.

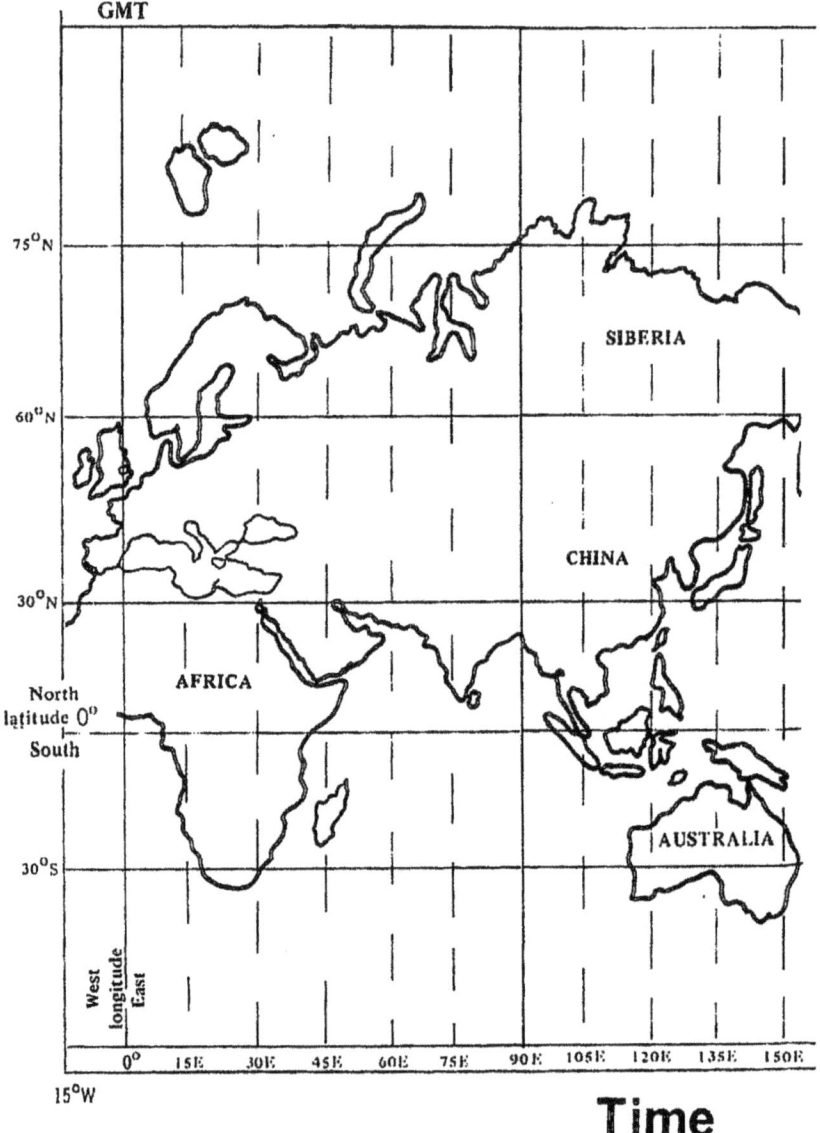

GMT

75°N

60°N

30°N

North
latitude 0°
South

30°S

SIBERIA

CHINA

AFRICA

AUSTRALIA

West longitude East

0° 15E 30E 45E 60E 75E 90E 105E 120E 135E 150E

15°W

Time

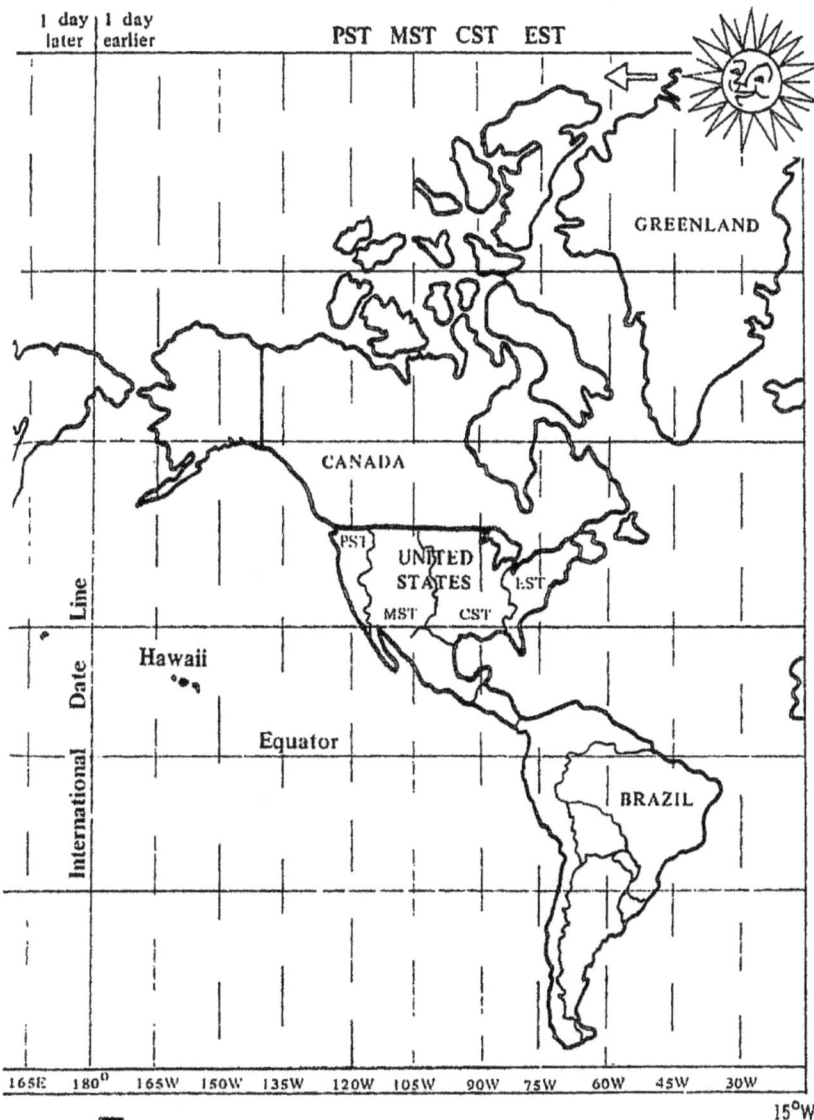

1 day later | 1 day earlier

PST MST CST EST

GREENLAND

CANADA

International Date Line

PST

UNITED STATES

MST   CST

EST

Hawaii

Equator

BRAZIL

165E   180°   165W   150W   135W   120W   105W   90W   75W   60W   45W   30W

15°W

Zones

TIME

Time

Anyone who has lived in open areas of the country knows the appeal of changing panoramas in the sky, the rising and setting of sun, moon, and stars. Glorious color in sunsets and cloud formations, thunder and lightning, rain and snow; all draw one's attention toward the skies. And in the crisp clear air of night, stars blaze and twinkle by the thousands, arousing a deep wonder and yearning to know what they really represent and are.

It is easy to imagine primitive man in his simple environment turning to the sky in daily wonderment and appreciation, watching the heavenly bodies move and change, gradually discovering the definite patterns being repeated, until after centuries of observation the wiser minds could make certain tabulations which enabled them to predict these movements in advance. Relics and records have been uncovered in all civilized areas of the world which prove the amazing accuracy of their observations, without instruments. It is shown they delved deeply into the study of the stars long before recorded history. The different areas of the world seemed to develop independent systems, no one can trace the dim distances they go back in time. Even the names of the constellations in use are prehistoric in origin.

It was important to their daily needs to keep track of the seasons, in order to know when to plant crops, or when to prepare for the coming of cold weather or times of flood. Without calendars, they had to count new moons, to learn that even this did not mark an exact year. In Egypt they watched for the rising of the great star Sirius at the summer solstice, for this showed the time at which the Nile river would flood—and their sustenance depended upon the Nile.

In some places, shadow poles were erected to show the exact time of noon when the shadow was shortest. These evolved into elaborately carved obelisks, or the "town clocks" of the ancient world. A circle drawn on the ground around this time-marker helped their priests to determine the time of equinoxes and solstices, as the length of the shadow changed at various times of year. Equinoxes and solstices were most important times of ritual, dealing as they did with patterns which involved the whole solar system, and these were used especially in sun worship. Sun dials based on a similar principle later came into use as ornamental garden clocks.

But the largest clock of all was the Big Dipper, an easily identified constellation which appears to revolve around the North Pole once every 24 hours, minus four minutes each day—the difference occurring because the earth not only turns on its axis in 24 hours, but is simultaneously moving forward a little on its path around the sun.

All the stars rise and set four minutes earlier each day, or two hours per month. In one year, this completes the full round or circle, and brings us back (almost) to the starting point. For this reason, we see a succession of different constellations in the sky at changing seasons of the year. This word "almost" is the Key to the "precession of the equinoxes," discussed on the next page.

The ancient used three successive types of worship, beginning first with stellar or star-worship, then lunar, and finally solar. Their systems for measuring Time evolved in the same order. The Pyramid at Giza is supposed to have been a stellar temple; later the Babylonians used a lunar month to mark their time; and still later Egypt made the summer solstice, the sun's longest day, a focus of their sun worship.

Egypt used a list of stars rising at 10-day intervals to mark off a ten-day week; but the Babylonians first introduced the seven-day week into Europe, counting off a list of 28 stars to observe the time, over 28 days.

The Chaldeans named the hours of the day for the seven heavenly bodies then known, in order of their distance from the earth— the day being named according to its first hour. In 24 hours, three of the seven planets were "left over," so the order of the days seems less logical than do the hours. They used Saturn, Jupiter, Mars, Sun, Venus, Mercury, and Moon, in that order to name the hours. The month always began with a Sunday following the New Moon; Sunday always began at the sunrise following a phase of the moon, or one of its four "quarters."

It is certain that Jesus was born before 4 B.C (most likely in 6 or 7 B.C.), because a known eclipse in 4 B.C. was historically recorded at the time of Herod's death. It has been said that all the mysteries of the divine incarnation of Jesus Christ, and "all the secrets of his wonderful life, from his conception to his ascension, are to be found in the constellations, and figured in the stars that announced them." He enacted a great solar drama; his life was itself a ritual, performed for the upliftment and salvation of Man.

PRECESSION OF THE EQUINOXES

PRECESSION OF THE EQUINOXES

Because the earth rotates daily on its axis, from west to east, the stars and sun appear to revolve around the earth, rising daily in the east and setting in the west. The earth also revolves around the sun once yearly so there is a larger cycle of this star-panorama spread out over the year. Add to this the fact that the earth wobbles on its axis like a top slowing down, due to the pull of the moon, so the Poles revolve in a conical path which carries the North Pole westward about 50" per year. This circular path which is completed in 25,794 years, or roughly the length of 26,000 years, is called the Platonic Year, or the Great Sidereal Year.

The star we now call the North Star is Polaris, the one toward which the North Pole is presently pointing, but this will progressively change over the next 26,000 years before the circle is back where it began, so in the year 14,000 the North Star should be Vega, due to the oblique angle the earth is tilted to its path of orbit.

For astrological purposes, the first point ("degree") of Aries is measured not by the appearance of the sun before a backdrop of the constellation of Aries in the sky, but at the moment the sun crosses the plane of the ecliptic, moving northward[1]. It is the date of equal day and night, "equinox," and this becomes our first day of spring. From the point of view of astronomy, the "plane of the ecliptic" is a plane passing through the center, or "equator," of the sun and extends outward to become the orbit of the planets. From the astrological point of view (that of an observer on Earth), the plane of the ecliptic traces the Sun's movement around the Earth over the course of a year against the background of stars. This is also the path of movement of the zodiacal constellations, the Moon and planets.

The vernal equinox slips backward, or retrogrades, about 50.2" each year, farther from the literal or visible constellation named Aries in the sky. (Most astrologers agree it has now preceded through Pisces into Aquarius.) Yet the actual potencies of each sign still have their effect according to the invisible zodiac, the signs being used, so it is likely that the true variations in the 12 types or personalities of people born in the 12 signs are less due to the distant seen constellations, than to some invisible pattern marked on the boundary of our own solar system.

Yet the distant constellations seem to affect the great Ages of Time. It is indeed true, that "there is more to the unseen than to the seen" worlds. The same holds true in the claim that there are a total of 12 planets in our solar system; two yet remain to be discovered.

---

[1] When the Egyptians and Greeks were beginning to write about astrology, the Spring Equinox point *was* lined up with the first degree of the constellation of Aries. Most astrologers assume this is why "tropical" (western) astrology continues to assign the first day of Spring (Spring Equinox) to Aries. But there may be more cosmic reasons for assigning the Spring Equinox to Aries as most cultures through time have designated this the "New Year" point.

AGES

AGES

During these periods, called Ages, religious worship takes the form of the appropriate celestial sign—that which the sun is said to assume as a personality in the same manner that a spirit assumes a body. "The 12 signs are the jewels of his breastplate, and his light shines forth from them, one after the other."

The ancient priesthoods of Egypt and Mesopotamia mapped out the 12 milestones or signs of the zodiac corresponding to the 12 months of the year, according to the "moving zodiac," so called because the first point of Aries moves continually westward due to this precession of equinoxes. These sections were called signs, and the priesthood named them after the apparent groups of stars, or constellations, in which the sun was rising and setting at that time. The Houses of the Zodiac became known as the thrones for the 12 Celestial Hierarchies.

Each Precessional Age is dominated by the characteristics of the constellation to which it is oriented. We know the Aquarian Age is here by this reasoning, yet no one has agreed on a date for its beginning. Their guesses range from 1762 A.D. through 2770 A.D. The reason for this is that there is not sufficient certainty about a past foundation from which to begin the calculations.

One of the favorite systems begins at the toe of Castor in 4699 B.C, and counting each constellation as 30 degrees would have brought the beginning of the Aquarian Age to 1844 A.D. That is probably very close, when we enumerate the many "Aquarian" events of the past 100 years, yet the time our country was founded had many Aquarian earmarks also, even to the Statue of Liberty.

AGE OF TAURUS

4699 B.C. should have marked the beginning of the Taurean Age, using this system. Taurus (the Bull) is a Fixed Earth sign, ruled by Venus. The nature of that Age was logically agricultural, with the principles of Mother Nature and earth goddesses emphasized. Cattle were both a valued asset and a symbol of worship. Wealth of the earth, metals and jewels were highly prized, the building of permanent structures such as the Great Pyramid and others were attempted—work which required Taurean attributes of great patience and determination. Taurus solidifies, and brings manifestation into its densest form, philosophically speaking.

We can always look to the priesthood to learn the dominant characteristics of an Age. They worshipped the sacred Bull at that time, when the sun was said to assume the body of Apis, or Serapis, and the Bull became sacred to Osiris. Jupiter at one time took the form of a Bull and carried off Europa thus. Hieroglyphic writing was invented in this Age and the use of papyrus substituted for clay tablets.

THE AGE OF ARIES

The Age of Aries was a time of war and conquest. The Babylonians, who were the first people to write from left to right, studied the stars quite profoundly and kept records. The Code of Hammurabi was established from an earlier compilation of Sumerian Law codes, and this became the basis of the Mosaic Law in this Age, which in turn has become part of our present-day laws. Law relates to Mars (ruler of Aries) in its aspect of severity and order. The Assyrians had an uncanny grasp of military tactics and strategy, and invented the most perfect military machine yet known.

Akhnaton introduced monotheism into Egypt (1375–1358 B.C.), but after his death the powerful priesthood restored their former patterns of worshipping the ancient gods. Alexander the Great captured Egypt in 332 B.C. Warrior nomads introduced the horse and chariot into Egypt; the four-wheeled cart was invented. The Euphrates civilization presented to mankind the religion of the priest kings. Outstanding were the Israelites with the symbol of the ram's horn, Moses, and the blood of the lamb on doorposts at the first Passover.

The civilization of Crete and Egypt rose and fell, while Greece inherited the glory of the eastern culture. The age of adventure and conquest ended in chaos, the Age of the Destroyer, Aries, following the Age of the Builder, Taurus.

Rome was founded in 753 B.C. The height of its military glory extended into the next Age, but it fully typified the idea of Aries and of Mars, even to worshipping their weapons of war.

THE AGE OF PISCES

The constellation of Pisces lies over the Atlantic Ocean, and the symbol of the Fishes itself is dual, one fish shown swimming upstream and the other downstream, so there is a pull between spirituality and reversion to lesser patterns, as well as the pull between the old and new at its European American shores. The older warlike struggles were retained in the sense that many wars took place in the name of religion, beginning with struggles between Hebrew and pagan, the Christian and Moslem, Jew and Arab, the Crusades, Joan of Arc, Catholic and Protestant, etc.

Pisces ruling the seas brought the Age of Navigation, when new lands were discovered and great sea battles were fought, when naval power meant authority. There was the building of Piscean institutions, of monasteries, hospitals, and such. Even the great cathedrals were Piscean, and the aesthetic qualities of the sign expressed themselves in great masterpieces of art and music. Drugs and alcohol, Piscean-ruled, came into commoner use during the Piscean Age.

When mankind descended like the Prodigal Son, as far into the dregs of life as he could go, this corresponded with the descent of creation into the Piscean Age on earth—the age of fishes—the fruit at the very bottom of the sea, or the lowest and deepest place on earth. Pisces rules the feet of man's body, and these are as far down as his body extends. Though the Prodigal once gave up his rights as son, he would prefer life as a servant in his Father's house to what he had descended into. So before him appears the Path, which must be traveled by foot, the Path of Return to God. Feet are the Pathmakers.

It is a long, slow journey before he will fall on his *knees* before his *father* (both ruled by Capricorn), sometime hence, but he will make it, and the interim of Aquarius promises some wondrous experiences, when Man comes into his own fulfillment, and use of his God-given powers.

Jesus' descent all the way from God into Earth, as the divine incarnation, was also as low as God could come to pick up mankind and carry him back onto the Path. As the feet are the farthest extensions of the body from the Central Self, so Jesus extended himself down into physical manifestation, and walked among the most humble. The feet are the only part of the body that habitually touch the earth, and are also our means of support and locomotion.

John the Baptist said he was not worthy to unlatch the boots of the Messiah (to uncover his *feet*, as a symbol of the Age). Jesus later washed the feet (only) of the disciples as a symbol of his mission to cleanse this part of archetypal Man. And the woman anointed his feet to prepare them for burial.

Just as we draw the light up through our bodies, beginning at the feet, the precession of the equinoxes evolves the earth upward from the Feet of the Macrocosmic Man, and will bring the Light of Christ higher until eventually in the vast ages ahead, it will reach throughout the whole Body of God. We have just begun—2,000 years ago.

AGE OF AQUARIUS

As for speculation regarding the Aquarian Age, we can use our own judgment. Aquarius rules electricity, air, space, the heavens, stars, invention, radio, electronics, airplanes, the ethers, change, unconventionality, the sudden or eccentric or unexpected. The very first word, "electricity" answers the question. It has not only been discovered, but put into tremendous use already, and Edison himself had an Aquarius Sun.

The planet Uranus, ruler of Aquarius, was discovered in 1781, just a few years before the birth of Benjamin Franklin, who later proved his theory about electricity in lightning (the symbolic flash of Truth) by use of a key—perhaps a key to the beginning of the Aquarian Age? Yet the two ages overlap for quite some time, as the twentieth century proved. No year could be named when one age ends and another begins. That would entail total destruction of the old in order to start anew, which has not occurred in our annals. It is obvious that Pisces and Aquarius have been overlapping throughout the twentieth and twenty-first centuries—the one decreasing and the other increasing.

Discovery of the New World brought as its first settlers people seeking religious freedom, freedom from conscription into armed services, or freedom from debtor's prison. But our planet was approaching the Aquarian Age when this drive toward freedom took place, as witness the several great revolutions around the eighteenth century for liberation from the hold of tyranny. Freedom from restriction is a Uranian characteristic.

That Piscean Age affairs continued on as Aquarius gradually moved in, we can still see, in the New Heaven and the New Earth being prepared and established under the noses of those still living in the Old. Drugs and alcohol; for example, are Piscean. But there will be a gradual disintegration of those and other Piscean tendencies as they become absorbed or broken down, and the whole trend of affairs will steadily take on the aspect of Aquarius. This transition between ages could take several hundred years to complete, since demarcations in the heavens are not precise. Their 30-degree divisions have been arbitrarily established by man.

The Aquarian Age promises the brotherhood of Man. Young folk have already begun to establish this in a primitive form, which their maturing leaders will gradually improve. The Age promises friendship and altruistic love of mankind, a time when ideals will find expression. It can't come too soon. Uranus is a "break-through" planet, and these are break-through times.

While God through Jesus touched His feet to earth in the Piscean Age, the energies of the Christ are harmonious with these times, since Aquarius rules electrical forces, the ethers and the heavens generally, and its opposite sign, Leo, in which it is reflected, is ruled by the Sun, involving solar energies and the Christ Light itself.

THE FOUR ELEMENTS

THE FOUR ELEMENTS

It is said the Cosmos has no need for the points of a compass, but as we come down into the world of manifestation, these do take on more significance. The four directions of space are usually correlated with the four Principles, or types of activity, having to do with the primary Creative Powers, and these in turn are called the Four Elements, or the four fundamental manifestations of nature, Fire △, Air △, Water ▽, and Earth ▽. Air or Space was mythically called the parent of the Sun (Fire), while Water was called the Mother or Matrix of Earth.

Fire, or Spirit, has the highest rate of vibration and is a great purging agent, the crucible in which impurities are burned out and modified or returned to the pristine state. It is the fiery quality of Light and regeneration, or **I AM**, and the Will-to-Be. It deals with the dynamic, directing Idea, or First Cause, and with Creativity. Characteristics of those who have planets in Fire signs are magnetism and enthusiasm, with animal spiritedness sometimes carrying them into difficulties. They may be prophetic, or irresponsible, or wildly idealistic. The Fire signs are Aries, Leo and Sagittarius. The elemental spirits associated with Fire are the salamanders. Michael is called the Archangel of Light (Samael sometimes of Fire).

Air: The ever-present but invisible forces of the universe are conducted via the quality of airiness, and Cosmic Consciousness is borne upon its wings. The flowering of mental activity into wisdom and knowledge comes about through the expansion of mind in concentrated thought; mentality is its tool. The Air signs are devoted to intellectualism, tending toward the abstract or philosophic view of religion, and attempt to classify the living intangibles which are unclassified. They may lack common sense and perspective. The Air signs are: Gemini, Libra, and Aquarius. The elemental spirits of air are called sylvans. The Archangel of Air and the realm of Mind is Raphael.

Water carries the quality of ductability and fluidity, acting as a flux in which are held the attributes of the life of all things. It is the soul essence which flowers in the seed of life. Its intense consciousness of feeling and sensation helps to perfect imaginative qualities. Habits and moods, along with a link to the past through the subconscious, sometimes arouse emotions which cause waves and undercurrents in the water. Those with a preponderance of planets in Water signs may keep some things submerged from sight, preferring to project an illusion. This trait also gives them a sense of wonder and interest in phenomena, magic and miracles. Depth of feeling may move them, and they must avoid being swayed from course. Nymphs and undines are the elemental spirits of water. Gabriel is the Archangel of this element. Water signs are Cancer, Scorpio, and Pisces.

Earth: The three preceding elements crystallize out into this fourth one, likened to the cube. Earth carries the quality of stability as shown by weight, hardness, and density. It is the mother of all material form, of flowering vegetation, jewels and mountain tops. Earth sign people have the consciousness of physical reality and tend toward the gradual attainment of perfection through physical experience and wise living. They have a tendency to substitute "good works" for inner spiritual development, and prefer the down-to-earth common-sense religions to the more profound aspects of divinity. They may become narrow or lacking in perspective. Earth signs are Taurus, Virgo, and Capricorn. Gnomes and pygmies are among the earth elementals. The Archangel of Earth is called Uriel.

Your sun sign alone gives but little idea of the proportions of elements in your makeup. It is not necessary to have a full birth chart to weigh the balance of the four elements on your birth date, but you do need an ephemeris for the day and year, and then convert the time listed to the time zone of your birth place. Simply read from the column the sign in which each planet was placed, and you can see which qualities of the elements are strongest, or lacking in your makeup. It is good to have a balance including at least one from each group. But don't worry, many good people don't have them all in one incarnation. This indicates the need to deliberately develop some of the missing qualities of those elements which were least prominent on your birth date.

The purpose of this book is not to show you how to set up or read a chart—information you can find in many books—but to help you get acquainted with the feeling and personality of the planets and signs.

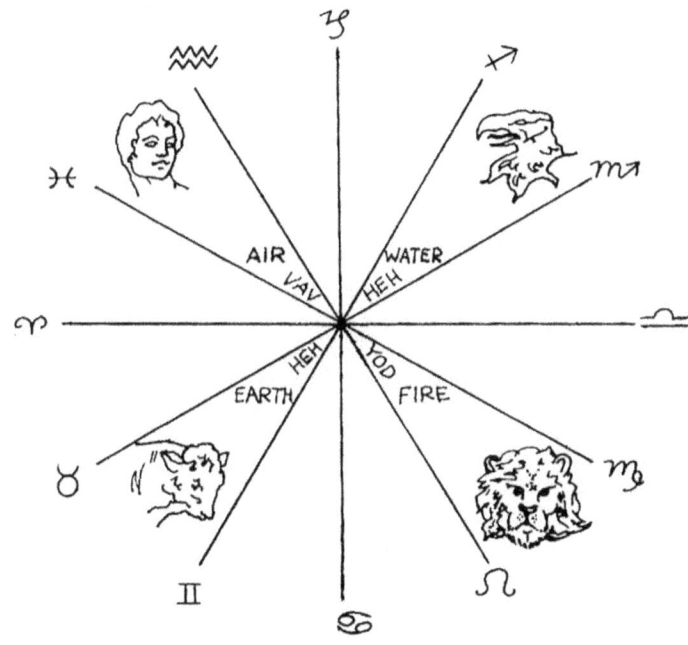

157

SIGN
LANGUAGE

Sign Language

The teacher was receiving his students, and he said to them:

"A person must overcome not only his earthly weaknesses, but also the tendency to identify himself with any one particular race, or any physical or personality trait. He must not confine himself to one nationality in consciousness. He has at some time been a member of many."

"Persons born in each sign of the zodiac have something they must rise above too, something that must be patiently overcome for spiritual growth. And each must remember that he is not of that sign, but he is just wearing it for one incarnation."

"Now what is it each of you wants most?"

ARIES said: "Let me lead the way into swift action and adventure. Something new and exciting."

Teacher: "Then, in order to achieve balance within yourself, you must cultivate the opposite. You need most to slow down, practice patience. Control that Fire; direct your energy in such a way as to inspire others to act in ways that are needed. Awaken them to new horizons."

TAURUS spoke then: "I want something substantial and secure, that I can depend on; property, money, or someone who loves me."

Teacher: "First you must overcome possessiveness, and learn to let go. Then all these things shall be added unto you. Become more flexible to change, and begin to detach yourself from the Earth element. It will take time, so enjoy life while accomplishing this.

GEMINI: "Give me change and variety. I want to learn something new today, then go on to another novelty tomorrow. By the way, what is this…?"

Teacher: "That's your curiosity sticking out. What you need to develop is stability and constancy. Tame the intellectual tempest and stick with things. No more will-of-the-wisp changes. However, you can provide the light touch for others through witty conversation and friendly companionship."

CANCER: "I want to go home, to enjoy some privacy with my family, and take care of some work in the house and yard."

Teacher: "Come out of your shell, and strengthen your inner balance, and develop less personal reactions. Direct that flow of running water. Try some management and organizational work, where you're looking after the well-being of humanity on a much larger scale."

LEO: "I want to express myself, and to display the results of my creative efforts, to enjoy the reactions of others."

Teacher: "Tame that ego and exchange your willfulness for the Will of God. You must learn unselfishness, then you may dispense the warmth of the Fire right from your loving heart. Teach this to children too."

VIRGO: "I want to work at a meaningful job, to serve. But I see some things around here that need correcting first."

Teacher: "Just for a moment, look up at the stars. Now rise above this environment and look down upon it in perspective. You should

162

cultivate larger horizons, stride above the small things of earth. And try to transmute negative criticism into wise judgment. Help us set up methods of working for those less meticulous than yourself to follow."

LIBRA: "I want a mate, or at least a harmonious social life, with everything smooth, intelligent and beautiful, with no bumps or wrinkles."

Teacher: "Alright, but don't depend on other people to fill your lacks and make you whole. You have to develop balance and completeness within yourself, and toughen those sensitive areas. Use your desire for balance and your fine sense of justice to bring peace to others about you."

SCORPIO: "I like to experience the very depth of things, and to probe the mysterious. But I don't want to talk about it."

Teacher: "Keep that temper and avoid jealousy and revenge, and your strength will carry you through. But use it altruistically, and not selfishly. Calm those stormy, emotional waters, and develop qualities which are useful in research, or long-range endeavor."

SAGITTARIUS: "I want to better myself, in any way possible—expand—nice things, travel, knowledge and experience.

Teacher: "It's fine to think big, but use common sense and don't overextend. Gather wisdom and inspiration from your travels and experiences, but learn as well to appreciate things close at hand and in nature. Spread good cheer, not merely from the pocketbook but from the heart."

CAPRICORN: "I want the top, success, respect, the pinnacle."

Teacher: "Come off that cold, earthly ambition 'trip' and, instead of prestige, strive for warmth of heart and humility. You must not overextend. Remember, in the spiritual life, up is down and down is up. Use your leadership abilities, not to advance yourself, but to lift others."

AQUARIUS: "I want freedom, brotherhood, innovation—just to be different."

Teacher: "Develop compassion and tolerance, and get rid of the obstinacy. You don't have to be all that unorthodox just to prove you are different. How about using your ingenuity to invent newer and better ways to help mankind toward a more liberated way of life?"

PISCES: "I want to live in a world of peace and compassion, filled with gentle consideration and love for those less fortunate."

Teacher: "Work on your confidence then, to shape up and grow stronger, and don't talk about things. There is strength in silence. Firm those emotional waters—don't let others sway you."

"And God bless you all."

NAME _____   BIRTHDATE _____

AUTHORITY

PHILOSOPHY

ALTRUISM

REGENERATION

BROTHERHOOD

CO-OPERATION

RISING SIGN

PERSONALITY

SERVICE

EARNINGS

CREATIVITY

COMMUNICATION

ENVIRONMENT

10 · 11 · 12 · 9 · 8 · 7 · 1 · 2 · 3 · 4 · 5 · 6

BIRTHPLACE _____   TIME _____ A.M. or P.M.

LAT. _____ LONG. _____   ZONE _____

                                        DAYLIGHT or STANDARD

ARIES	TAURUS	GEMINI	CANCER	LEO	VIRGO	LIBRA	SCORPIO	SAG.	CAPRI.	AQUAR.	PISCES
♈	♉	♊	♋	♌	♍	♎	♏	♐	♑	♒	♓

ELEMENTS	PLANETS		
CARDINAL			
FIXED			
MUTABLE			
FIRE			
AIR			
EARTH			
WATER			

		☉	☽	☿	♀	♂	♃	♄	♅	♆	♇	ASC	MC
☉	SUN												
☽	MOON												
☿	MERCURY												
♀	VENUS												
♂	MARS												
♃	JUPITER												
♄	SATURN												
♅	URANUS												
♆	NEPTUNE												
♇	PLUTO												
ASC	ASCENDANT												
MC	MIDHEAVEN												

www.ingramcontent.com/pod-product-compliance
Lightning Source LLC
Chambersburg PA
CBHW051524120626
46551CB00012B/1071